SONIA BOYCE

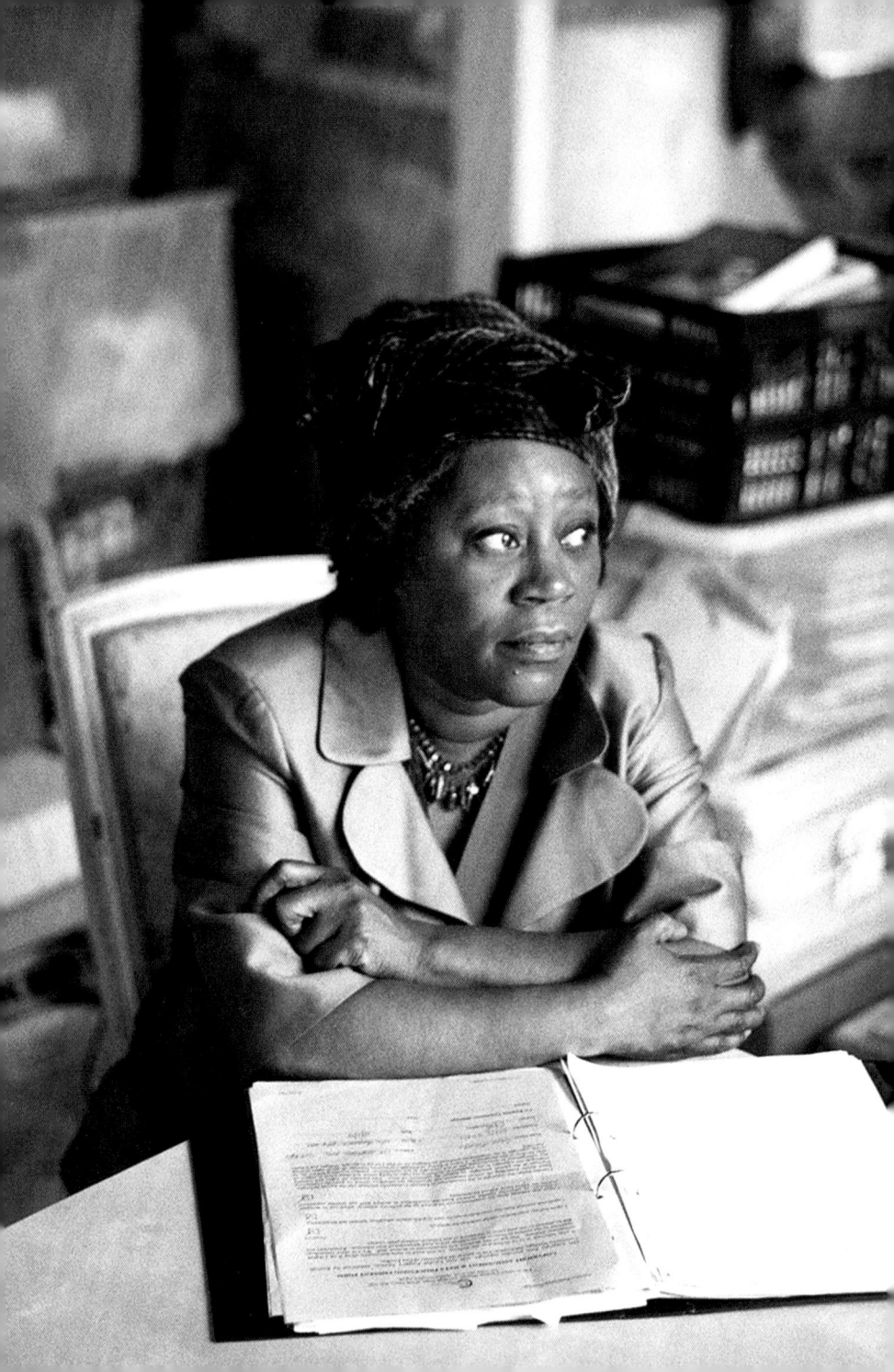

SONIA BOYCE

ELENA CRIPPA

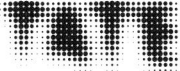

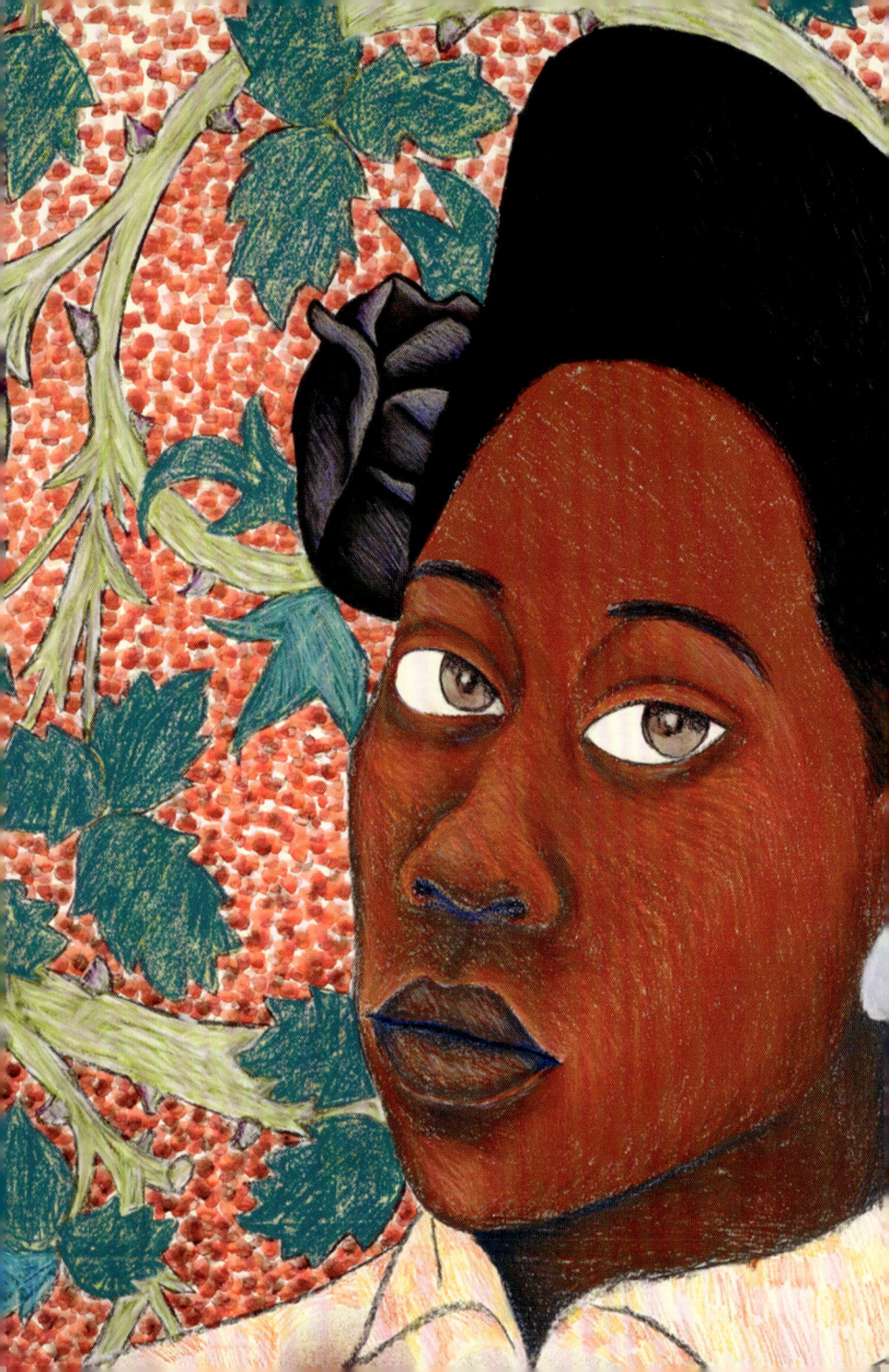

In her large pastel *Big Women's Talk* 1984 (p.6), Sonia Boyce rendered the vibrant colours and clashing patterns she experienced in her own childhood home and the homes of other families of Caribbean heritage. The juxtaposition of these patterns conjures the interweaving of multiple experiences and identities. As the womenswear designer and curator Christine Checinska has noted, it underscores the key role that textile and wallpapers played in bridging postwar British and Caribbean culture, spurring a sort of creative creolisation of 1960s swinging London.[1] The central figure in *Big Women's Talk* is the artist as a child: nestled in her mother's lap, she listens intently to her talking with friends, storytelling being traditionally a female activity. The child's gaze is both intent and dreamy. Is she already aware of the relational and political implications of listening and carrying those stories? Can she foresee that one day she will not only hold these stories dear but take them into new trajectories as she shapes a story of her own?

Boyce's mother and father met shortly after arriving in London in the 1950s from Barbados and Guyana (then British Guiana) respectively, and Boyce, who was born in 1962, grew up in the capital's East End. As a child, Boyce drew incessantly. From the age of fifteen she attended weekly life drawing classes at East Ham College of Art and Technology, where she later undertook her Foundation course in Art and Design (1979–80). Empowering representations of Black women were absent from the media of that time as much as from art history, and at home Boyce started making self-portraits, explaining: 'I needed to see myself.'[2] She went on to study Fine Art at Stourbridge College in the West Midlands (1980–3).[3] The tutors, many of them associated with conceptual art, were white and male;[4] as was common at the time, female students were not taken seriously, and Boyce's tutors did not know how to handle the referential nature of her work.[5]

Boyce's true art school training took the form of a personal engagement with feminism and rare visits she and other students arranged with female tutors, including the artists Margaret Harrison and Susan Hiller. Boyce admired Hiller's work, her engagement with feminism and surrealism, and her transgression of the tenet – by which students at Stourbridge, as in many art schools, were expected to abide – that intentions should and could be articulated.[6] Of Harrison, Boyce said: 'She

Lay Back, Keep Quiet and Think of What Made Britain So Great 1986 (detail, see pp.46–7)

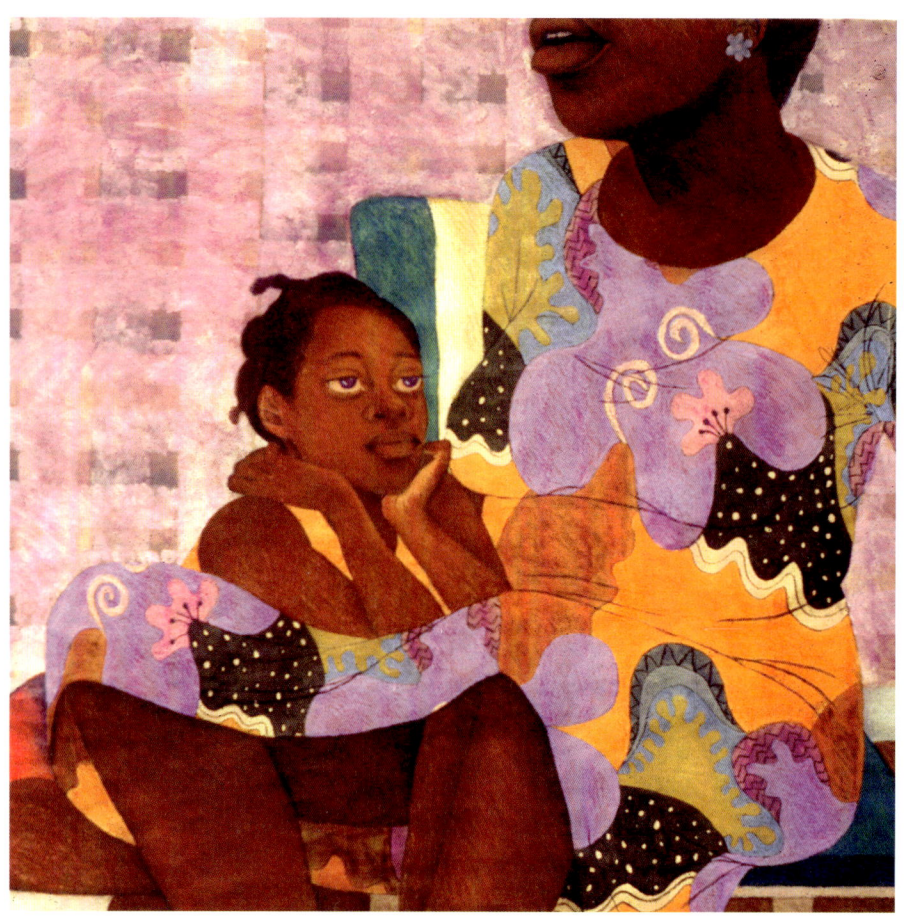

Big Women's Talk 1984
Pastel on paper
122 × 122

taught us that even rape can be a subject for our canvases –
sexual abuse, abuse of trust, abuse of power, an everyday
occurrence, a highly political act.'[7] As a young student, Boyce
had already embraced the mantra 'the personal is political'.
However, in the 1970s and 1980s, mainstream feminism failed
to address and challenge racism.[8]

In 1981 Boyce saw Wolverhampton Art Gallery's *Black Art
an' Done* (opposite), a rare exhibition of the work of young
Black artists, including Keith Piper and Eddie Chambers. The
exhibition was part of a broader effort to create a network of
Black artists at a time of growing unrest resulting from police
harassment of Black communities. The following year, the
group behind *Black Art an' Done*, the Pan-Afrikan Connection

(later renamed the BLK Art Group) organised the First National Black Art Convention (p.8), which Boyce also attended, at Wolverhampton Polytechnic.[9] These events proved pivotal for many artists, who forged long-lasting friendships and found a forum to discuss their work and the form and function of Black art in Britain. Additionally, the group represented a powerful form of cultural activism against institutional racism, which led to art galleries beginning to open up to the presentation of Black artists' work.

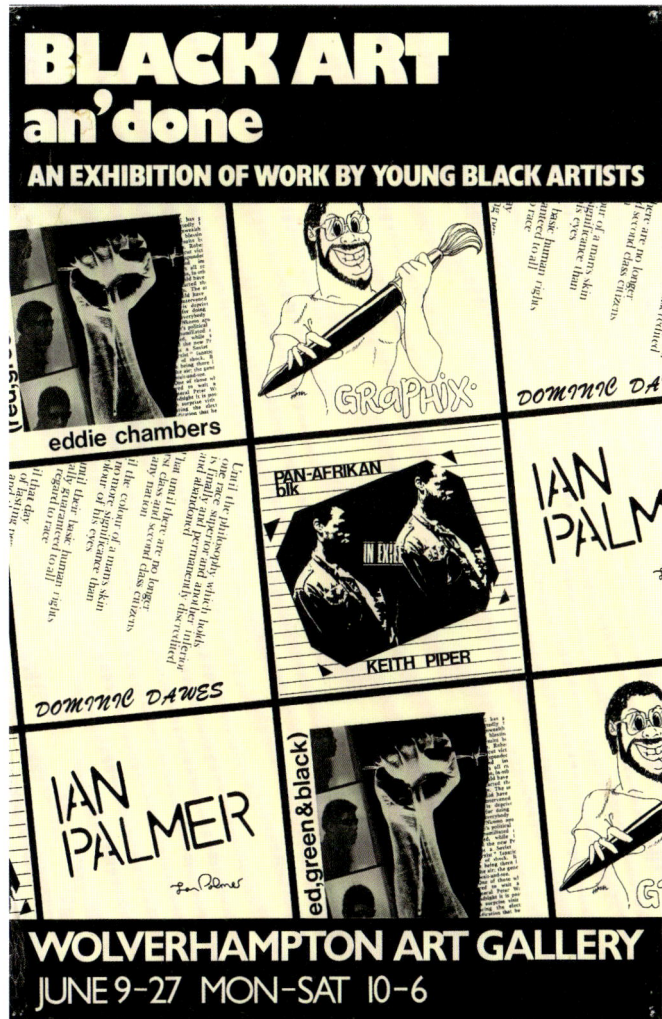

Poster for the exhibition *Black Art an' Done*, Wolverhampton Art Gallery, 1981

Despite the prevailing collegiality, women artists were a minority at the First National Black Art Convention, and had limited scope to raise their voices and defend their positions.[10] The few female participants – among them Boyce, Lubaina Himid, Claudette Johnson and Marlene Smith – ended up gathering separately, and felt empowered to address their experience as women with an African and Caribbean background growing up in the UK. Boyce exhibited her work publicly for the first time in 1983 at London's Africa Centre in the first of many exhibitions curated by Himid, who fought back at the widespread perception of Black women artists'

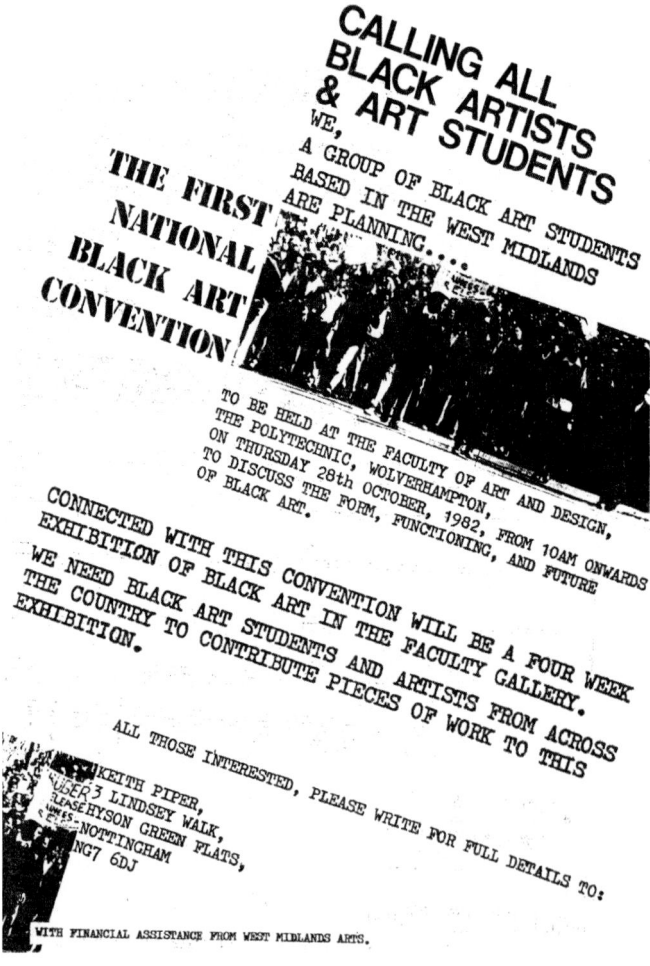

Poster for the First National Black Art Convention, Wolverhampton, 1982

work as negligible and exotic and its exclusion from major exhibitions, stating: 'We are claiming what is ours and making ourselves visible.'[11] Among the other exhibitions Himid curated was *The Thin Black Line* at the Institute of Contemporary Arts (ICA), London in 1985, which included work by Sutapa Biswas, Boyce, Himid, Johnson and Ingrid Pollard, among others. The exhibition presented artistic practices that bridged the divide, then common among feminist artists, between theory-based conceptual practices and the figurative representation of personal, embodied experiences.

Boyce was involved in early feminist art discussions about medium and representation. At the time, painting existed as a sort of gladiatorial arena in which artists – mostly men – had to prove themselves through the resoluteness and unique quality of their paint handling.[12] Declining to step into an arena in which women could occupy only a subaltern position, Boyce, like Claudette Johnson, adopted the traditionally humbler medium of pastel. She knew, too, of the American-French painter Mary Cassatt, who employed pastel as it started regaining popularity in 1870s France. Cassatt used pastel in her intimate representations of women and children, and understood the choice of medium as sociopolitically rooted in its association with the domestic sphere and female predicament.

Boyce explained: 'A child's curiosity and a fear of the adult world, religion and personal relationships: these have been my main themes. The familiar/sensual, the familiar/uncomfortable.'[13] This tension between the familiar and the burdens of social and family life and expectations is the subject of *She Ain't Holding Them Up, She's Holding On (Some English Rose)* 1986 (p.45), whose main figure defies women's traditional representation as delicate and ultimately fragile. Boyce's is not just a remarkable self-portrait in terms of likeness but in the performative staging of inner and poised strength.

Earlier in 1982 Boyce had seen for the first time the work of Frida Kahlo, who had her first retrospective outside Mexico at the Whitechapel Gallery, London.[14] It was a profound and validating encounter: in her work Boyce, like Kahlo, would connect her personal, situated experience to broader cultural and social dynamics understood from a feminist perspective. She did so in a way that was representational yet addressed inner, unconscious feelings as much as outer appearance.

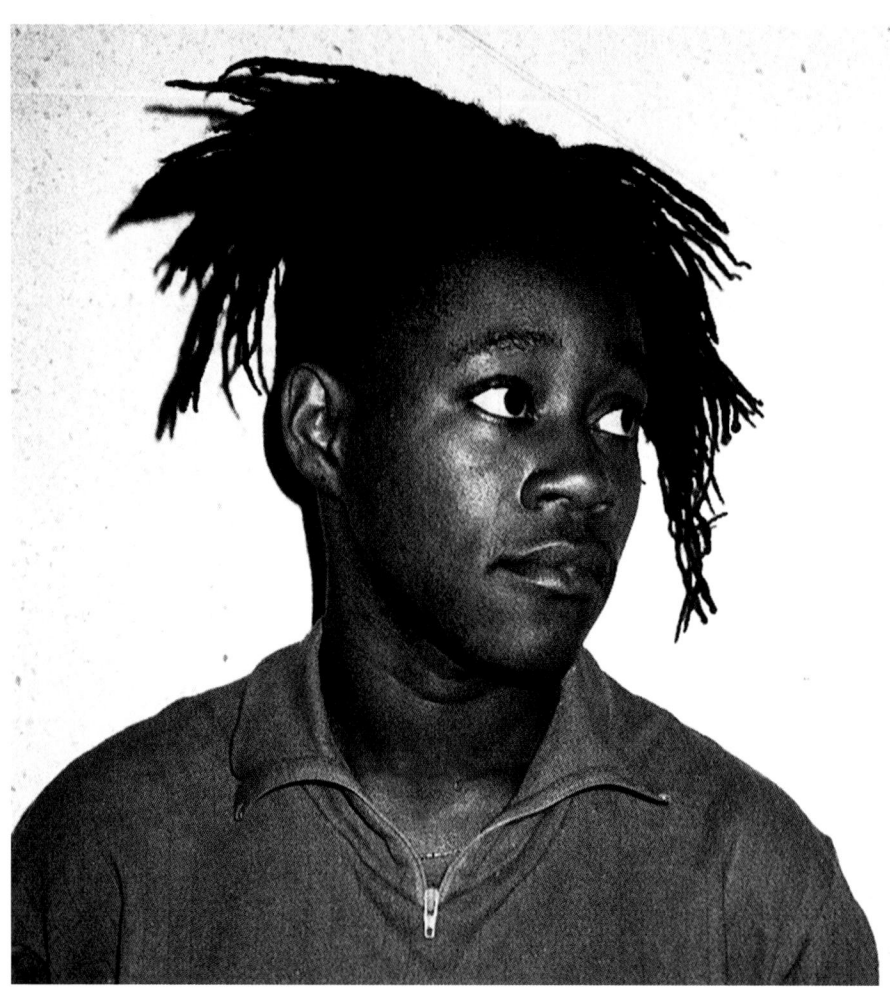

Pogus Caesar
Sonia Boyce, Handsworth,
Birmingham 1983
From the series *Represent*
Digital gelatin silver print
35 × 25

Boyce has referred to Kahlo's canvases as 'circles of strength',[15] and there is no doubt that her early self-portraits share with Kahlo's a performative stance in which identity is constructed and deconstructed in a socialised, affirmative manner that was rare in the representation of women.

As a student, Boyce had also started researching wallpaper designs. These designs furnished her scenes with a sense of domesticity and saturated the picture plane. In *Missionary Position II* 1985 (pp.42–3), the background is a light pink wallpaper of repeated patterns reminiscent of art deco fan motifs; the confined interior is furnished with a sofa

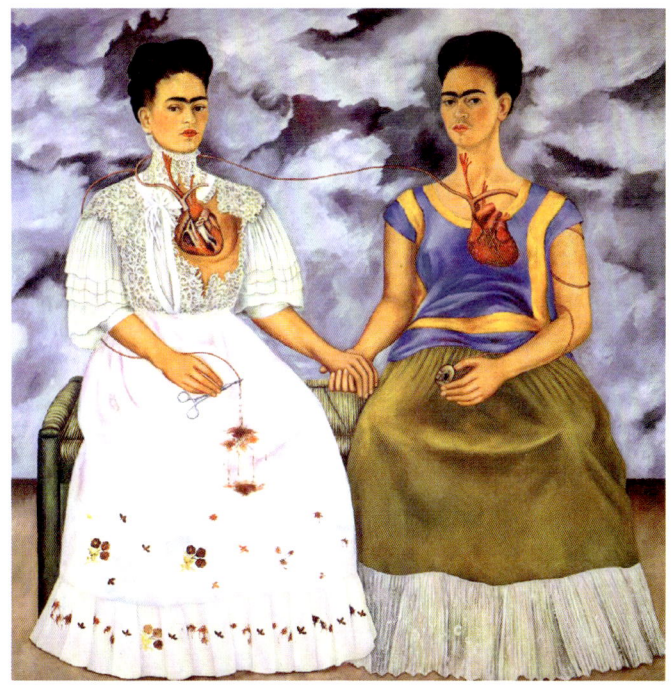

The Two Fridas 1939
Oil paint on canvas
174 × 173

and side table lamp that give the picture a sense of staged homeliness. The pastel is a direct reference to Kahlo's *The Two Fridas* 1939 (above), a double self-portrait in which one figure is dressed in formal, sober attire and the other in folk clothes.[16] Boyce, too, represented herself twice. On one side she appears composed, praying with her eyes closed and wearing sharply cut clothes. On the other, wearing a red headwrap and dress, she spreads out in a sensual pose with her eyes open and her arm reaching out in a gesture that seems to both recognise and reject her other self. While all the elements are drawn convincingly, their fragmented nature creates a sense of disjunction and unsettledness. Mystery and desire, the whimsical and the onerous, are brought together in an arresting and elusive image.

The combination of photographic image and text was a dominant mode at art school. In Boyce's work, too, the text started to enter the picture. *Missionary Position II* is inscribed as follows: 'Laard but look my trials nuh – / they say keep politics out of religion / and religion out of politics / but when were they ever separate? Laard give me strength'. The use of patois reflects and contests the culture and values Boyce assimilated growing up, while the inscription and title stand for historical and contemporary forms of white oppression encompassing the role of white Christian missionaries in imposing colonial rule. The failure to address the dark history of the British Empire is central to another pastel work, *Lay Back, Keep Quiet and Think of What Made Britain So Great* 1986 (pp.46–7). Over three of four panels, crosses inscribed with the words 'Cape Colony', 'India' and 'Australia' float against the drawing of a wallpaper inspired by a design of rambling roses by the artist and designer William Morris, whom Boyce admired for his socialist and activist ethos. The roses here are black rather than Morris's red, but red stains the white background. On the last panel, a self-portrait of the artist gazes out at the viewer, linking historical events to contemporary experiences.

In the 1980s, Boyce read extensively American authors such as James Baldwin, Toni Morrison, Audre Lorde and Alice Walker, leading her to the writer and anthropologist Zora Neale Hurston. These authors played a crucial role in articulating the Black experience both intellectually and viscerally, in ways that readers might not simply understand but feel in their bodies. As these writers did, Boyce addressed the transgenerational trauma that linked contemporary life to the brutal and dehumanising experience of colonialism and slavery. Referencing the strong African and diasporic storytelling tradition, Boyce has described herself as an 'oral translator through pictures', explaining: 'I gather things up which I remember, as a means of going forward to make certain cultural and political points. I'm making visible the warmth, as well as the confrontation of our daily lives as the basis upon which things can be discussed.'[17]

COLLAGE, PHOTOGRAPHY & AN EXPANDING THEORETICAL HORIZON

Boyce has referred to her love of René Magritte as a 'guilty pleasure.'[18] Adopting collage's strategy of creating unexpected or uncanny associations among disparate elements, the Belgian artist connected objects to words and pictures to titles in incongruous or contradictory ways. Collage is an intimate activity that allows new images and new meaning to be created out of an act of destruction – the cutting or tearing of existing material. In her works on paper, Boyce deployed collage strategies to similar ends, making the familiar disturbing or surprising, and posing questions about the nature, conventions and soundness of representation. As she has remarked: 'Collage gave me space and taught me the meaning of defending oneself.'[19]

Boyce started making collages as a student, using cut-outs from *Ebony* magazine to explore Black women's relationship with their bodies.[20] She has continued drawing on the creative potential of collage throughout her career, including in works produced in the late 1980s that exploited what the art historian Kobena Mercer describes as the possibilities afforded by collage and montage: of 'articulating an anti-essentialist understanding of black identity' and heightening our awareness that all cultural identities are composed.[21]

One of Boyce's most iconic works started as a collage. *From Tarzan to Rambo: English Born 'Native' Considers her Relationship to the Constructed/Self Image and her Roots in Reconstruction* 1987 (pp.14–5) was preceded by a small work combining photo-booth self-portraits of the artist with fragments from cartoons and magazines. The photographs and cut-outs were then enlarged and worked with paint, crayon and ink, developing into a work measuring over three metres wide in which six photographic portraits of the artist are repeated and arranged alongside popular racist caricatures from children's books depicting a native man and golliwog figures. The title made reference to the main character of a hugely successful series of movies, the first of which was launched in 1982. Boyce, who engaged with film theory and studied the construction of Black stereotypes for audiences' consumption and assimilation, was fascinated by the popularity of Tarzan and Rambo, white characters who could survive and thrive in the jungle, bearers of beastly qualities that white supremacy had routinely attributed to Black people to justify their oppression. *From Tarzan to Rambo* can ultimately be interpreted as addressing whiteness: the experience of partaking willingly or unwillingly in the daily re-enactment of prejudice and exclusion, and the construction of a world of white superiority that debases and hardens.

Boyce's career had risen rapidly. In 1986, she held her first solo exhibition at AIR Gallery, London. In 1987, when she was twenty-five, her work was acquired by Tate, and in 1988 she had a solo exhibition at the Whitechapel Gallery. She recognised the difficulties of being thrown into the limelight, and the need for change: 'I think I need to get away from it

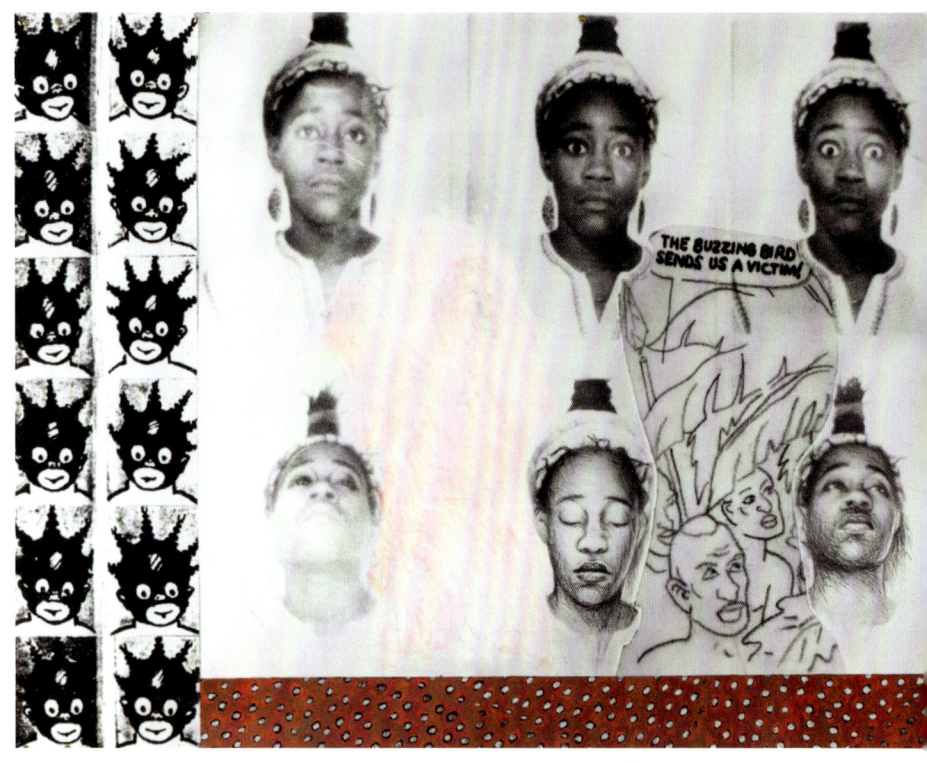

THE BUZZING BIRD
SENDS US A VICTIM

From Tarzan to Rambo: English Born 'Native' Considers her Relationship to the Constructed/Self Image and her Roots in Reconstruction 1987 Photographs and photocopies on paper 125 × 360

being so intimately personal, or appearing to be so intimately personal.'[22] Although she had positioned her experience centrally in her work to address subject and identity formation from a situated position, she did not want her work to be reduced to her image. Additionally, Boyce – alongside such artists as Keith Piper and Sutapa Biswas – occupied a difficult space between the impulse to portraiture as a means to give visibility to the Black experience and a wish not to essentialise that experience. As the literary and cultural studies scholar Ian Baucom noted, such a position involved finding a way 'to both shoulder and shrug' what Kobena Mercer called 'the burden of representation' – the expectation that these artists' work should speak to the entire Black experience.[23]

Soon after making *From Tarzan to Rambo*, Boyce's work began to shift rapidly, from focusing on the Black presence to investigating it as an object of representation. Boyce was living in a shared house with other artists. They worked alongside one another and often improvised collaborative endeavours

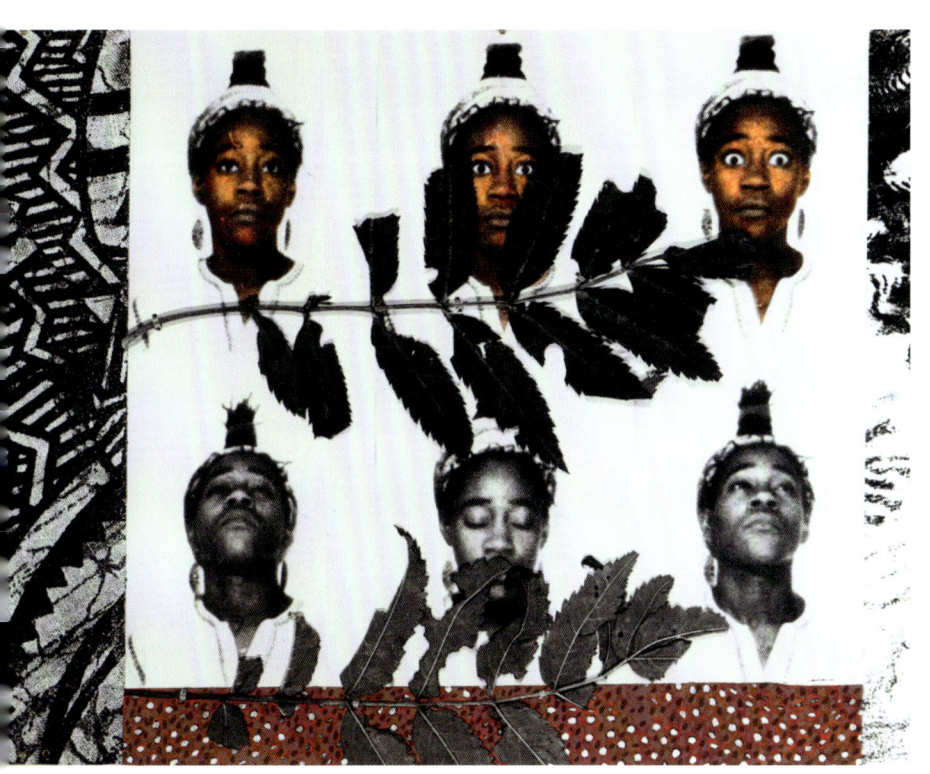

that had a lasting influence on Boyce's work, instilling in her
a fascination for what happens when people come together
and create without preconceived expectations. The house had
a dark room, and Boyce met regularly with artists working with
photography, among them Maxine Walker, Rotimi Fani-Kayode
and Ajamu X. She had already encountered her future life-
partner, David A. Bailey, a member of the D-Max photography
group. Bailey collaborated with the film and video collective
Sankofa and went on to co-edit, with the cultural theorist
Stuart Hall, a crucial 1992 issue of the photography magazine
Ten.8 subtitled 'The critical decade: Black British photography
in the 1980s'. Boyce participated eagerly in the burgeoning
photography discourse, which articulated many of the politics
of the constructed image she addressed in her own work.

Boyce was and remained committed to critical theory,
engaging with queer theory, sexual politics and gender
performativity as much as postcolonial studies. She was close
to the critical forum created in 1994 with the foundation

of the Institute of International Visual Arts (Iniva), which sought a space of enunciation beyond the dichotomy of centre and periphery.[24] Alongside academics and curators such as Kobena Mercer and Gilane Tawadros, Boyce aimed to enable the discussion of Black artists' works beyond narrow identity traits. In 1995, she and the artist Zineb Sedira founded the Black Women Artists Study Group as a site for exchange with fellow artists. Pollard was part of the group, which operated between 1996 and 1998, and Ain Bailey, Zarina Bhimji and Johnson were among the artists who gave presentations.

BODY, TOUCH & THE FURNISHING OF ENCOUNTERS

In 1987, Boyce worked with Martina Attille on the design of her film *Dreaming Rivers* (1988) (opposite), which told the story of Miss T., who journeyed from the Caribbean and settled in England in the postwar period. Boyce meticulously planned the sets of two interiors, Miss T.'s bedroom and living room, contributing to a meditative work on migration, dislocation and intergenerational relationships.

Boyce's work soon moved from the staging of intimate settings to the exploration of the boundaries of private and public spheres. In 1990, she participated in the exhibition *The Invisible City* at the Photographers' Gallery, London, for which she created *The Photobooth* and *The Ticket Machine* (pp.52–3). As curator David Chandler discussed in the exhibition catalogue, these works hinged on 'the physical tensions of the city – the body confined and in transit', and developed 'an interplay between private and public spaces', between anonymous collectivity and singularity.[25] At the push of a button, the ticket machine of the latter work dispensed postcards addressed to 'My dearest'; written in a diaristic tone, they expressed intimate feelings or offered future scenarios involving pleasure and danger. The photobooth's interior combined mirrored surfaces with Boyce's collaged imagery of domesticity. These spaces were both comforting and bewildering, as possibilities of access, intimacy and comfort were by turns suggested and frustrated.

The same year, Boyce realised *Pillowcase* 1990 (pp.54–5), which collages excerpts of text imprinted on cotton in different colours. The texts were taken from lonely hearts ads: intimate desires and expectations broadcast in newspapers by individuals hoping to be found and loved. In 1992, when Camden Arts Centre commissioned Boyce

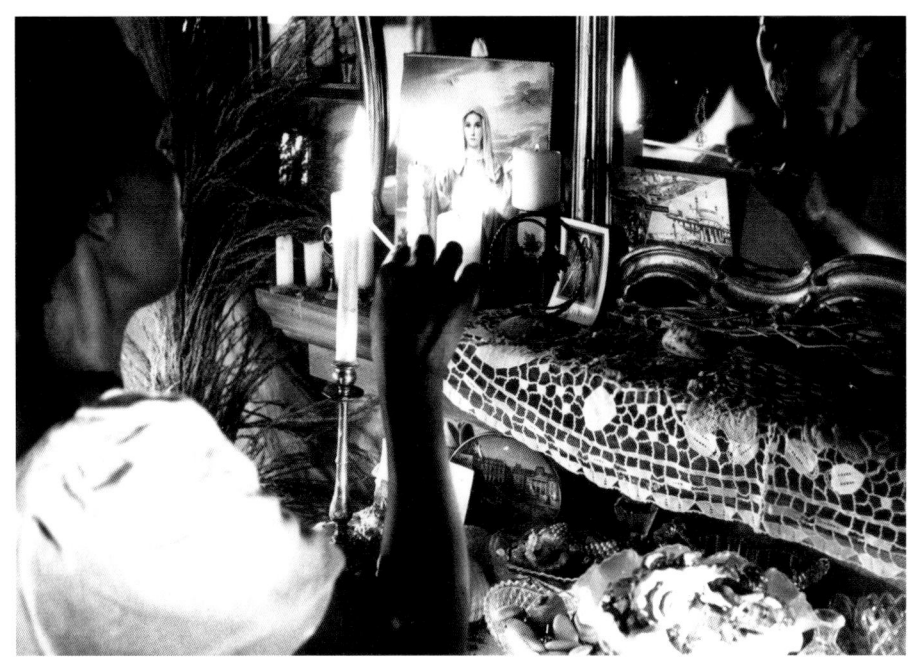

to develop a new project as part of the public art project Northern Adventures, she adopted a similar strategy of making the intimate public. The site was the British Rail tea rooms at the busy London St Pancras Station, for whose tables Boyce created 4 *Tablecloths* 1992. These cloths, imprinted with a floral design, are inscribed with snippets of dialogues, some reworked from film scripts, revealing hopes and fears about recent or forthcoming encounters.

Two years after its initial realisation, *The Photobooth* found a new incarnation as part of the 1992 installation *Is It Love That You're After or Just a Good Time?* (p.19) at Ikon Gallery, Birmingham. Visitors were invited to enter a confined space with a rubber floor lined with reflective, crinkled silver curtains and a mirror-ball suspended from the ceiling. The work nods to Andy Warhol – both his studio, the Factory, which was covered in silver paint and foil, and his *Silver Clouds* 1966 (p.18), floating balloons shaped as pillows with which visitors were able to interact. Boyce's piece, too, called for or at least suggested interaction, offering strangers the possibility of establishing proximity and finding love – or, at least, to be present with others – in a space of whimsical beauty.

Martina Attille
Dreaming Rivers 1988
16mm film
31 mins, 7 secs

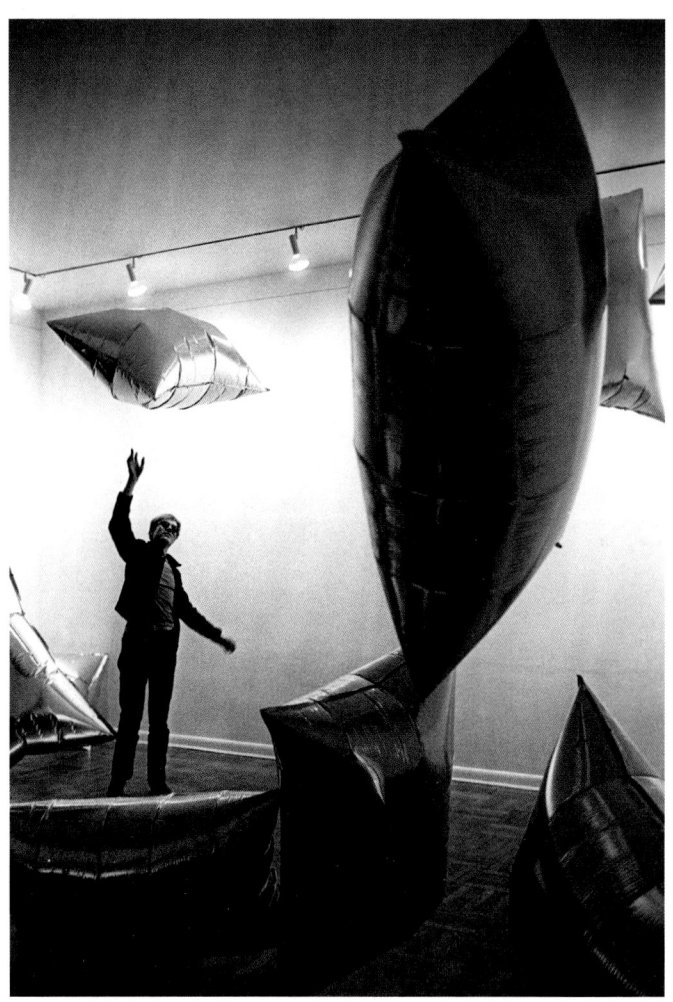

Andy Warhol and Billy
Kluver (contributor)
Silver Clouds 1966
Installation view, Leo
Castelli, New York

*Is it Love That You're After
or Just a Good Time* 1992
Miralon, rubber and
mirrorball
Dimensions variable

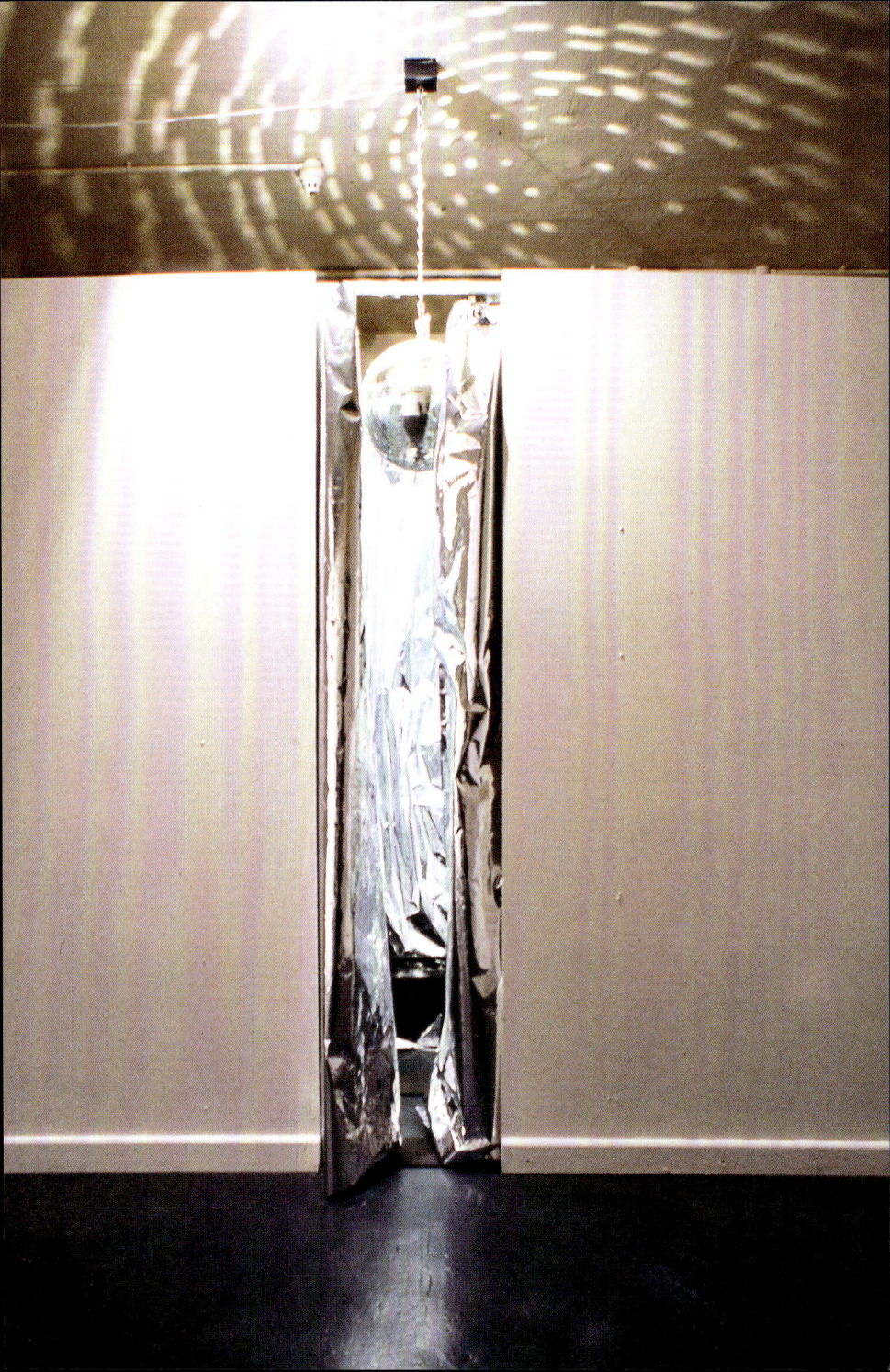

HAIR SCULPTURES

In 1993, with no preconceived ideas about their status, Boyce began making small sculptures out of hair. These works emerged from what she described as a desire to touch and be in touch with materials in a way that was not mediated by the photographic or other processes.[26] She went on to make larger pieces with hair extensions bought from Afro-Caribbean hair shops: in *Plaited and Sewn with Red Satin Belly* 1993 (p.57), dark braided hair is sewn into a red piece of fabric, while *The Comforter* 1993 (p.56) has braids of dark hair arranged into a rounded shape from which two cylindrical forms protrude.

The styling of Afro-textured hair has been a political subject as much as a personal choice for centuries. Women of colour have had a complex and changing relationship with their hair, whether containing it to try to fit in or pushing back by allowing it to grow unrestrained; during the civil rights movement, for example, the combing out of hair became a public statement of resistance as part of the 'Black is beautiful' movement. Tending to hair has a special role in parents' nurturing care of their children, but there is also the licence people take in touching others' hair – a form of microaggression that specifically affects people of colour.[27] Boyce's sculptures made of hair engage with all these histories and the multitude of deep-seated desires and assumptions connected to them.

Boyce first presented around thirty sculptures made of hair as part of the 1993 solo exhibition *Do You Want to Touch?* (opposite) at 181 Gallery, London, inviting viewers to manipulate them. Gilane Tawadros convincingly draws a connection between Boyce's works and the 'relational objects' of the Brazilian artist Lygia Clark: not manifestations of the artist's self but rather means for viewers to become aware of their expressivity in the role of participants.[28] Undoubtedly, these works also bear a relationship to surrealist sculptures, found and altered objects that often elicited both desire and repulsion, such as Méret Oppenheim's iconic *Object* 1936 or Mimi Parent's *Masculin Feminin* 1959 (p.22) for which, playing with cross-dressing and the fetishist power of hair, the artist refashioned her own hair into a man's tie.[29]

If Boyce's hair sculptures look fetishistic, Ian Baucom argues that they are, in fact, 'frustrated fetishes': most of them are not made of natural hair and, as such, are deliberately counterfeit.[30] They suggest that the body is doubly missing – in both its physicality and its meaning – while the hair's

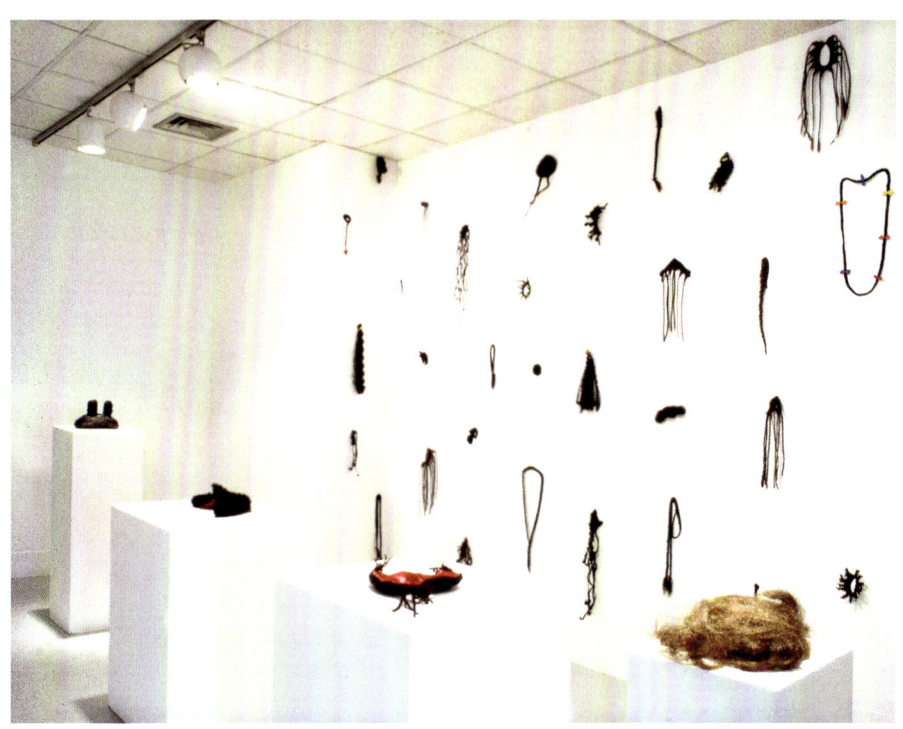

synthetic quality raises questions around representation and authenticity, and hints at the constructed, hollow nature of the identity these objects are meant to emanate from. In a way that recalls Magritte's work, Boyce's hair sculptures seem to open up the space (and question the relationship) between signified and signifier, disturbing the impulse to name and classify.

In 1998, Boyce reflected: 'Much of my recent work has to go close to the body. Close to those areas of the body that are loaded with cultural significance.'[31] She wanted to 'explore how an identifiable fragment of the African Diaspora subject is imagined as a body that contains excessive meanings'.[32] It could be speculated that in moving closer to the body, Boyce was moving further from language – from what the French philosopher Michel Serres described as its power to enclose the world into a rigid system of codes and narratives – in order to recuperate open-ended exchanges through objects.[33] By allowing visitors to touch her sculptures, Boyce furnished haptic, visceral experiences that could act as springboards for querying entrenched meanings, assumptions and practices.

Do You Want to Touch? 1993
Installation view,
181 Gallery, London

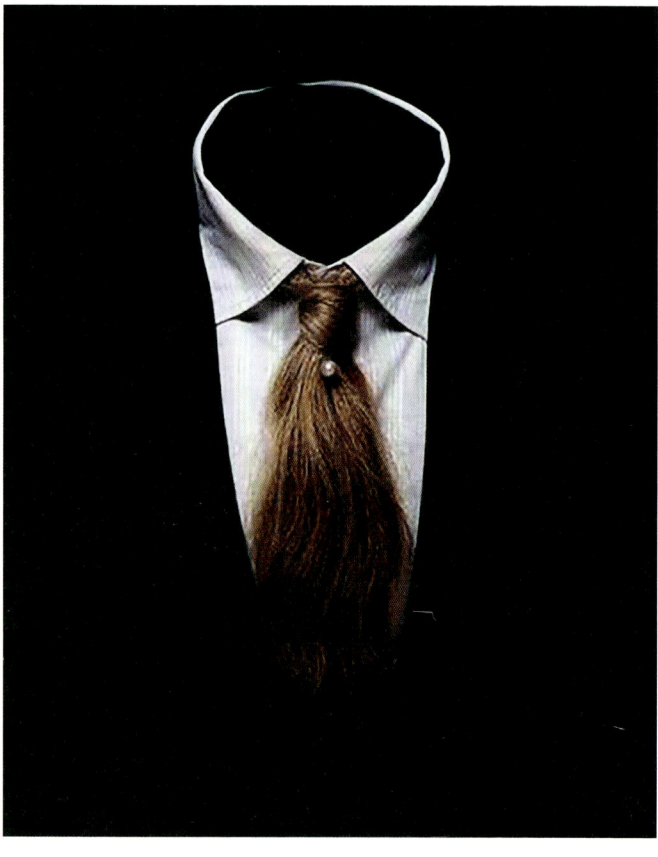

In 1994, Boyce participated in a group show organised by the collective Bank at BANKSPACE, a disused London warehouse. Titled *Wish You Were Here*, it took the form of a group of domestic-style spaces. Boyce contributed *Afro Blanket*, a 'blanket' of hair woven from numerous Afro wigs, laid on a bed in one of the spaces designated as 'bedrooms' (p.59). She also presented *Clapping Wallpaper* 1994 (p.58), a wallpaper created by silkscreening two photographic images of clapping hands which alternate down the length of the paper, like a film strip. The intimacy of the domestic setting and the sense of overt acknowledgement hinted at by the clapping hands combined to blur, once more, the private and public spheres – and possibly to suggest the futility of such a distinction.

Also in 1995, London Printworks Trust, a not-for-profit workshop and studio complex, commissioned artists to make work for the *Portable Fabric Shelters* exhibition, whose theme was global migration and the conditions faced by refugees and the homeless. Boyce made a group of works, including *Tent*, *Blanket* and *Umbrella* (pp.60–1). The first was a camping tent bearing enlarged reproductions of an ear and surrounding facial hair; around the edge of *Umbrella*, Boyce printed the brows and closed lids of a pair of eyes, while *Blanket* was a large piece of cotton silkscreened with the detail of a face – eyebrows, eyes and nose. These works seemed to act as possible shelters and cocoons in which to enter into contact with someone else's deeply personal experience.

Two large-scale photographs of the time also show details of body parts: *Head I (Skin)* 1995 (p.62) depicts a short beard and dark hair growing from a scalp and face, *Head II (Dread)* 1995 (p.63) long dreadlocks. Another photographic work, *Three Legs of Tights Stuffed with Afro Hair* 1994 (p.64), shows stitched tights from which dark hair protrudes. These images seem to hint at abjection – the segregation of body parts from a full sense of self, and their reduction to unruly and possibly threatening elements. The art historian Linda Nochlin observed that artists' representation of fragmented body parts is linked to the experience of modernity and its associated loss of wholeness and connection to a sense of place and natural rhythm.[34] At least since surrealism, the representation and assemblage of body parts has also acted as a means of questioning sexuality and the body as unified entities.[35] In these works as well as in her hair sculptures, Boyce by turns isolates and stitches together fragments of biological and synthetic body parts in what can be interpreted as transgressive acts towards the questioning of the markers of unambiguously gendered and racialised bodies.

Other photographic works brought intimacy to public settings. *Untitled (Kiss)* 1995 (p.65), commissioned by Iniva for the ICA exhibition *Mirage*, saw a wall of the gallery covered with a large-scale print of two people, a woman of colour and a white man, nearly touching in a kiss. For one of the site-specific projects that were part of the exhibition *Cottage Industry*, organised by the independent art space Beaconsfield, London in 1995, Boyce realised *They're Almost Like Twins* 1995 (pp.66–7), printing two large black and white photographic portraits of her friend, sound artist Ain Bailey, with different exposures and installing them on the gallery's windowless rear exterior wall where they were visible from the street and a passing rail line (opposite). The tightly cropped portrait shows Bailey's hands holding and squeezing her face into a pronounced pouting expression – a playful act, but one that exaggerates her full lips in a visual echo of a racist stereotype repeated endlessly in European and American caricatures. Both works, featuring photographs blown up and placed in public spaces, would have been highly sensual encounters that could have disrupted a sense of normalcy around the representations of stereotypes and construction of identities.

Boyce's most ambitious project to deal with hair dates from 1997, when she was invited to be the first artist in residence at Manchester University and realised a project at Cornerhouse, then Manchester's contemporary art centre. The artist placed an advertisement in the Cornerhouse publicity brochure under the playful banner: 'Have you ever thought that your face was a work of art? Then read on …' Over fifty people responded to Boyce's invitation to visit Cornerhouse, don a synthetic Afro wig and be photographed. Rather than remaining a detached observer, Boyce talked to her subjects, who began to analyse the meanings they attached to the Afro hair.[36] The performance of identities and meanings linked to the Afro, and the discussions that took place between the artist and the predominantly white participants, functioned to question the stereotypical and changing characterisation of Black identity. Many of the hundreds of photographs Boyce took that day appear in the installation that resulted from the project, The Audition 1997 (pp.26–7), which features multiple portraits of each sitter, both with and without the wig.

In the video work Exquisite Tension 2006 (p.29), the artist Richard Hancock and the curator Adelaide Bannerman – who had never met before – have their hair plaited together by Boyce in front of the camera. The work evokes other performances involving the restriction of movement and the fastening of two people: Boyce has said that it directly references Art/Life One Year Performance 1983–4 (p.28), also known as 'Rope Piece', for which the artists Tehching Hsieh and Linda Montano spent an entire year bound together by a rope tied around their waists. Exquisite Tension is also reminiscent of a collaborative work by Ulay and Marina Abramović, Relation in Time 1977, a seventeen-hour performance in which the couple sit back to back, tied together by their hair. Boyce's

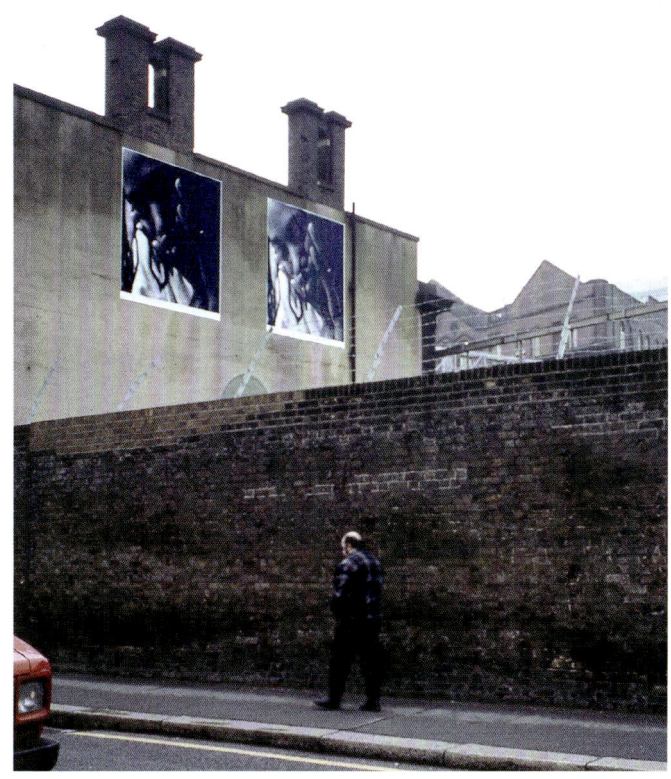

They're Almost Like Twins
1995, as installed on
the exterior wall of
Beaconsfield, London
(see pp.66–7)

work, however, is not about endurance but the artist's role in staging an encounter and the entanglement of differences and commonalities between two individuals with different hair textures and skin tones. Hancock later recalled the experience of being tied to Bannerman as relaxed and calming, but felt that 'The physical construction of the image is so overt that I think it could be read as "hyper-raced" and "hyper-gendered", and, continuing on this path, "hyper-heterosexual"'.[37]

Hancock's statement seems to suggest an uneasiness in reckoning with his race, gender and sexuality. Addressing an individual's whiteness, masculinity and presumed heterosexuality can elicit discomfort, since each reveals the underpinning ideologies and unquestioned power structures that have historically been positioned as objective and also neutral.[38] Additionally, white people often treat the invitation to explore their racial subjectivity as a charge of racism that must be rebutted. *Exquisite Tension*, with its representation

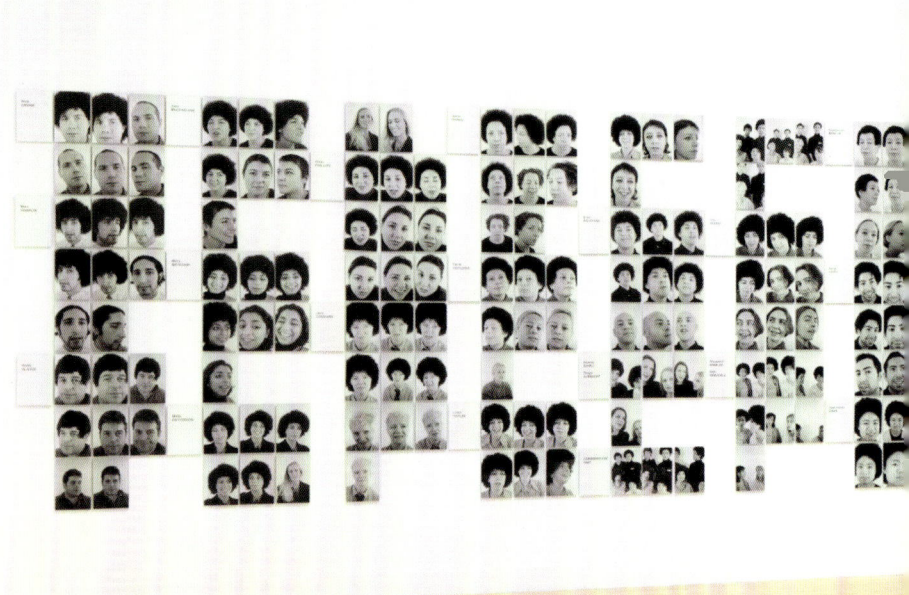

of entangled experiences, could be seen to elicit patterns of encounter and transformation that invite a reflection on the role each of us plays in the collective construction, reproduction and negotiation of identity. What does Black look like? What does white look like? Such critical questions, played out every day, are not universal but relate to one's individual history and inheritance – and Boyce's work asks each viewer to address these questions from their own situated position.

LISTENING & MAKING PUBLIC

As the architecture historian Mark Crinson has noted, Boyce appears uninterested in the notion that art emanates from a singular voice or viewpoint.[39] Instead, she seems drawn to art as an exploration of the place of the subjective within the collective. Many of Boyce's works reveal the role of public interactions in challenging personal assumptions, and provide frameworks for encounters and exchanges where participants renegotiate individual agency within the collective.

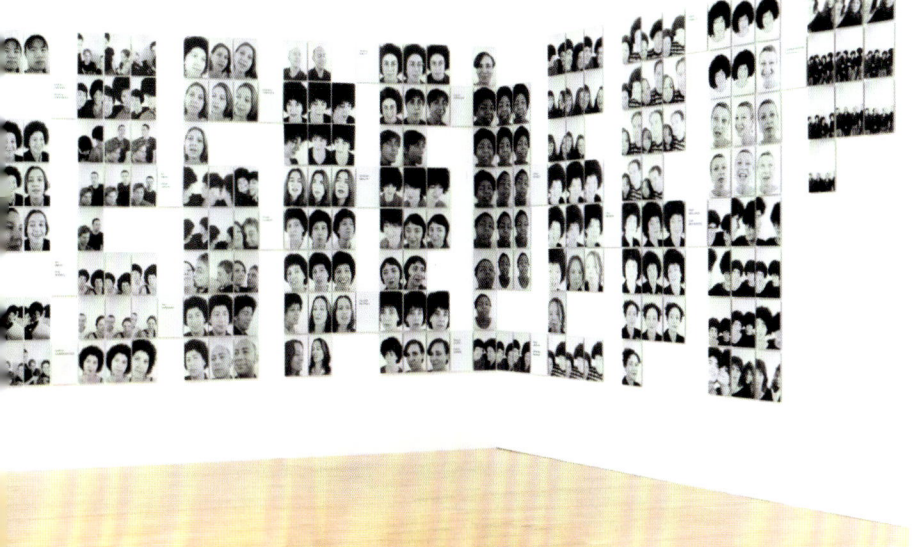

The Audition 1997,
printed 2018
390 photographs; C-prints
on paper, face-mounted
to acrylic glass
Each 30.1 × 20.1 × 1.4
Installation view,
Tate Britain, London, 2019

In 1964, Andy Warhol purchased a Carry-Corder, the newly available portable cassette recorder, and started recording his friends and colleagues, urging them to recognise inner adversities as collective issues. For Warhol, interiority was not a stabilising sense of self but a burden, and sound was about evading the containment of privacy.[40] Like Warhol, Boyce has made use of sound's spatial expansiveness not to seek aesthetically groundbreaking performances but to explore the voice as located in the moment of listening, in the public and collective realm, and to offer the possibility of undermining the isolation of listeners' interiority, as one becomes absorbed with others.

Many of Boyce's works since the late 1990s have used music, sound and dance to renegotiate and transform the private sphere. One of the earliest is the *Devotional Collection*, a collective memorialisation of the contribution of Black British female musicians to transnational culture, which takes

27

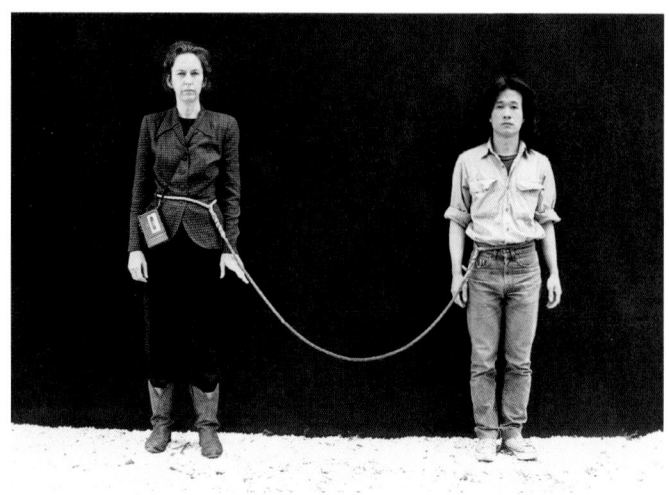

Tehching Hsieh and
Linda Montano
Art/Life One Year Performance
1983–4, New York

the form of an ever-expanding collection of material culture
including CDs, cassettes, vinyl records and other ephemera.
It began in 1999 when Boyce held a workshop in Liverpool
with a group of women, and they began reflecting on the first
records they ever bought. When Boyce asked the participants
to name a Black British female singer, their limited capacity
to recall the names of the women whose voices contributed
profoundly to British culture led to a project about collective
memory and music, which developed out of an ongoing
dialogue with friends and the general public.

In 2007, invited by the National Portrait Gallery to develop
a new project, Boyce staged *Devotional*, which brought together
photographs of eighteen singers from the National Portrait
Gallery's collection alongside a hand-drawn installation
created over two weeks. Using carbon paper, ink and pencil,
Boyce wrote out the names of singers then drew a series of
concentric lines and patterns around them, as if their very
names were resonating; each set of reverberations expands
outwards until they encounter and become connected to those
of surrounding practitioners. In 2008, Boyce turned this wall-
based installation into a wallpaper (pp.86–7), which she has
since shown as part of the installation *Devotional Wallpaper and
Placards* 2008–18, in which placards resembling those held at
demonstration marches, covered in printed photographs and
texts celebrating Black women from the British music scene,
lean against walls papered in *Devotional Wallpaper* (pp.84–5).

Oh Adelaide 2010 (pp.74–5), a collaborative work by Sonia Boyce and Ain Bailey, incorporates found film footage of the American-born jazz singer Adelaide Hall. Before moving to the UK in 1938, Hall was a significant figure in the Harlem Renaissance, and her vocalisation on Duke Ellington's record 'Creole Love Call' (1927) introduced what became known as scat singing: a wordless technique where the voice mimics a musical instrument. Hall appears throughout the work, performing on stage, illuminated and engulfed by an animation of dazzling white light that threatens to dematerialise and obliterate her image. Bailey's soundtrack combines reworked audio tracks featuring Hall and other performers from the *Devotional Collection*, underscoring how her voice is historically situated and part of an ever-changing experience of listening and remembering.

Since at least the 1970s, feminist works by writers as diverse as Donna Haraway and Audre Lorde have utilised voice as a crucial metaphor in treating the expression of gendered, racialised and queer identities.[41] The concept of polyphony – or a plurality of voices – was adopted as a metaphor in

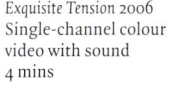

Exquisite Tension 2006
Single-channel colour
video with sound
4 mins

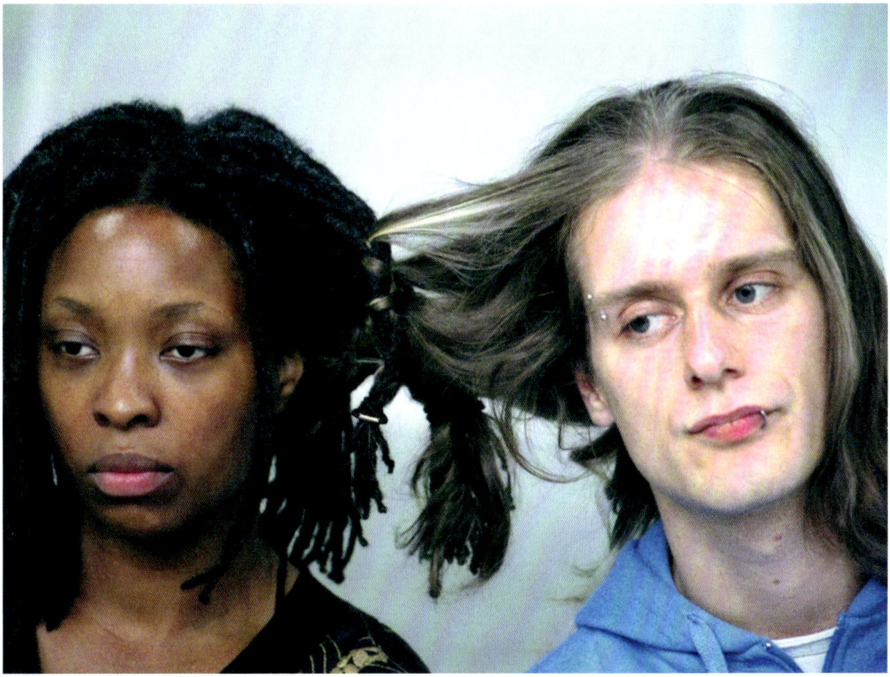

literature (Mikhail Bakhtin) and postcolonial studies (Edward Said) as well as in feminism, to purpose language as malleable, embodied and dialogical, the expression of a multiplicity engaged in a collective and collaborative action of co-creation. It is not surprising given her position as a Black woman invested in feminist, postcolonial and queer studies that Boyce's work has directly engaged literally, metaphorically and aesthetically with the voice and, as we shall see, with polyphony.

PARTICIPATION: THE SELF & THE COLLECTIVE

Since the 1990s, Boyce has consistently worked in a participatory manner. Turning viewers from observers into collaborators is a distinctive aspect of twentieth-century and contemporary art, although the term 'participation' itself has been used rather loosely to cover a broad terrain. The art historian Claire Bishop has highlighted three concerns that have motivated artists to encourage participation since the 1960s: to create an active subject whom the experience will empower, to foster a non-hierarchical form of collective creativity, and to create a sense of communal experience and social responsibility.[42] Boyce's work shares these aims, which she has pursued by seeking participants not to complete given tasks or take on predetermined roles, but to partake in the shaping of open-ended endeavours.

Boyce's participatory projects often rely on institutional invitations and the artist's willingness to engage with the specificity of each context. In 2007, the invitation came from the Ruskin School of Drawing & Fine Art, University of Oxford. In the austere setting of the University's Magdalen Chapel, Boyce orchestrated an unlikely collaboration between sound and voice artist Mikhail Karikis and Alamire, an ensemble of consort singers inspired by medieval and early modern choral work.[43] Karikis's sound work pitches his fractured vocalisations against a version of the Renaissance-era sacred a cappella 'Tu solus qui facis mirabilia' by the fifteenth-century composer Josquin Desprez, its score reworked and tempo modified. To begin with, Karikis's vocalisation is dissonant and discordant and pushes the polyphony towards the antagonistic. As the work progresses, however, Karikis employs more melodic vocalisations and the relationship between solo and choral singing moves from seemingly adversarial to dialogical, even playful.

The project entailed a working process that has become typical of Boyce's more recent collaborative practice: having set the parameters of the situation, she steps back from any directorial position to observe the activities and dynamics of exchange as they unfold, enabling the participants themselves to negotiate their roles and contributions. In this way, the work calls not just for collectivity but for individual agency reclaimed and enhanced as part of collective experiences.

The performance resulted in the three-screen installation *For you, only you* 2007 (pp.72–3), in which Boyce's moving images frame Karikis, the ensemble and ensemble director David Skinner against the backdrop of the single-nave church. As viewers and listeners, we shuffle between the ensemble and the soloist, and between different delivery modes. By engaging his body's resonant cavities, Karikis produces a wide range of utterances, his non-linguistic vocalisations recalling dada sound experiments such as Kurt Schwitters's phonetic poem 'Ursonate', as well as the jazz-scat of Ella Fitzgerald and other musicians.

Having made *For you, only you* and *Oh Adelaide*, Boyce realised that her interests in jazz-scat and dada were connected, as the two had historically influenced each other as well as popular music more broadly.[44] The two forms pushed back against what the American artist and composer John Cage described as the military quality of language; in his view, syntax, which orders words into meaningful sentences, 'is the arrangement of the army. So what we're doing when we make language un-understandable is we're demilitarizing it, so that we can do our living.'[45] In later works, Boyce continued to work with other practitioners to pursue what she has referred to as 'improper language' and 'non-harmonised sound' as musicalising forces: acts of resistance that disturb the social order shaped by the prescriptive meaning of established forms of linguistic communication.[46]

For *Dance of Belém* 2011 (p.32), another three-channel video installation, Boyce invited a musician and a dancer to respond independently to the Praça do Império gardens in Belém, a popular location in Lisbon. DJ Johnny Cool Train produced a soundtrack inspired by kuduro, a culturally hybrid genre of electronic dance music originating in Angola, following the country's liberation from Portugese colonial occupation, and sampling different traditions, from soca to techno. The

Dance of Belém 2011
Three-channel video
installation with sound
7 mins, 7 secs

moving images show Lisbon-based dancer Vânia Gala moving and looking around at herself and others with unapologetic confidence, then following, approaching and mimicking the posture and behaviour of sightseers and passersby.

Boyce has referred to the influence on her work of American artist Vito Acconci. Beginning in 1969, Acconci developed performances in the public sphere that eliminated the distinction between the space of the performance and that of the viewer, testing what degree of proximity and interaction might be experienced as acceptable or confrontational. *Dance of Belém* tests the same barriers from the vantage point of knowing how the Black female presence has historically been seen and how it affects others in a predominantly white environment. Here it engenders an act of resistance, Gala's performance seeming to embody a refusal to be held in place by other people's perceptions and expectations. Boyce's subsequent single-channel video *Move* 2013 (p.76), commissioned for the Göteborg International Biennial of Contemporary Art, references both Sweden's illegal cultural nightlife scene of the 1980s and the 2001 anti-globalisation protests. Like *Dance of Belém*, this work foregrounds dancers

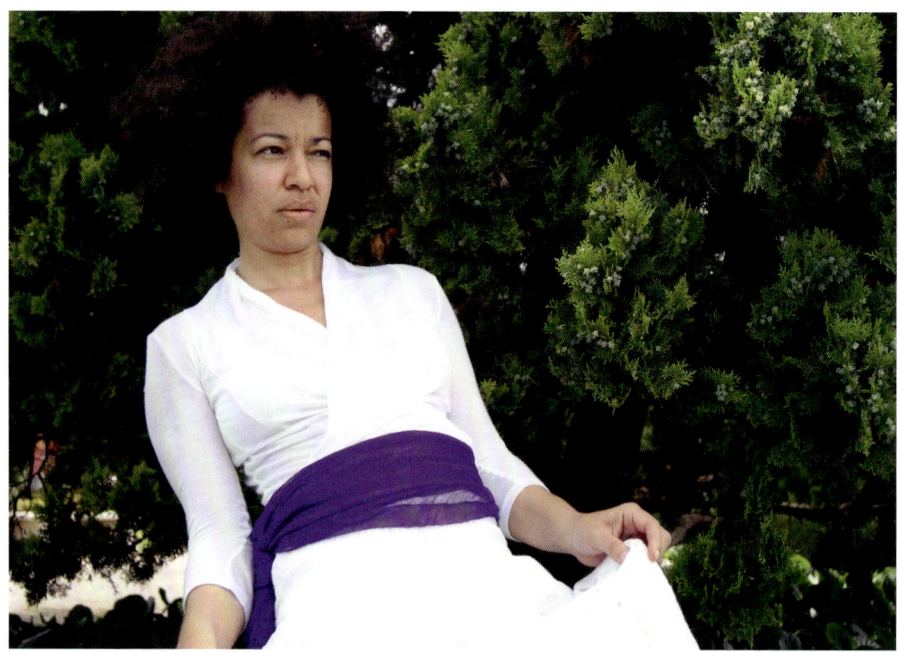

and club revellers who, through their physical presence and interaction, give expression to forms of resistance that push against the limits of social acceptability.

Boyce commonly arranges for the participatory events she organises to be documented through photography, film and audio recording. Following the event, she turns to this documentation to produce works to be presented in gallery settings. Of this process, she has said: 'I recoup the remains of these performative gestures – the leftovers, the documentation – to make the art works, which are often concerned with the relationship between sound and memory, the dynamics of space, and incorporating the spectator.'[47] As the art historian Jean Fisher observed, although Boyce's procedure does not eliminate power relationships, 'it provides a model for reflecting critically on the multiple, shifting positions of artist and viewer, receiver, maker, finder, producer, consumer, analyst or catalyst'.[48]

Exquisite Cacophony 2015 (p.77) was produced for the 2015 Venice Biennale at the invitation of curator Okwui Enwezor. The projected video documents a live event at the Gamble Room in the café of the Victoria and Albert Museum, London, featuring improvised exchanges between two vocalists Boyce invited to perform in front of an audience: the Minneapolis-based freestyle rapper Astronautalis and the London-based, classically trained experimental vocalist Elaine Mitchener. Astronautalis interacts with the spectators, who hand him cards on which they have previously written topics for discussion; a few minutes into the film, Mitchener – having until then stood among the audience – begins interrupting Astronautalis's performance with a vocal act before joining him on stage. The two continue interacting in different styles, one with fast-paced, rhythmic deliveries, the other vocalising, producing utterances and stretching sounds and pauses. Boyce has emphasised the anarchic impetus in Astronautalis and Mitchener's concurrent vocal forms, which produces 'an exhilarating cacophony: a discordant clash of sound fights for its own conjoined coherence'.[49]

The moving-image installation *We move in her way* 2017 (pp.82–3) originated in an event Boyce organised at the ICA in 2016, in which Elaine Mitchener and Barbara Gamper, improvising vocals and movements, were joined by dancers Eve Stainton, Ria Uttridge and Be van Vark in a performance staged and filmed in front of an invited audience (pp.80–1). Audience members wore masks, allowing them to engage the performers without feeling exposed, and as they manipulated objects and textiles and approached, touched and moved alongside or with others, the dynamics and roles of audiences and performers shifted. Boyce subsequently edited the footage and sound recordings of the performance into a seven-channel moving-image installation. Each screened and projected image shows discrete aspects of the event and is displayed at a different scale and angle, such that visitors can only apprehend the overall work by moving around and stitching together different takes and perspectives.

We move in her way is a particularly ambitious work, underpinned by the artist's willingness to allow it to develop beyond her control. The masks worn by audience members are a collage of Boyce's hair and a reworking of *Dada Head* 1920 by the artist Sophie Taeuber-Arp, itself an appropriation of Oceanic sculpture. By referencing Taeuber-Arp's work, Boyce summons its subversive impulse to push against the moral, cultural and institutional monitoring of the body, its behaviour and language. The open-ended nature of the participants' involvement, meanwhile, was inspired by the work of Lygia Clark, who remarked: 'True participation is open and we will never be able to know what we give to the spectator-author. There no longer is the object to express any concept but the spectator who reaches, more and more profoundly, his own self.'[50] Interdisciplinary free improvisation can be a liberating experience, an encouragement to being in the moment with no expectation about presupposed outcomes or traditional notions of what is aesthetically acceptable.[51] It also requires participants to be attentive to and trust others, to be vulnerable, and to engage jointly not just in performing together but in devising how to be and act together.[52]

This and other participatory works by Boyce recall *Funk Lessons* (opposite), a performance the artist Adrian Piper carried out in collaboration with small and large groups between 1982 and 1984. Piper, who rehearsed with participants not just basic moves but the language of funk as a means of communication and self-expression rooted in the music of the African diaspora, explained that the resulting performances were not about how participants looked or what they achieved but rather 'how completely everyone participates in a

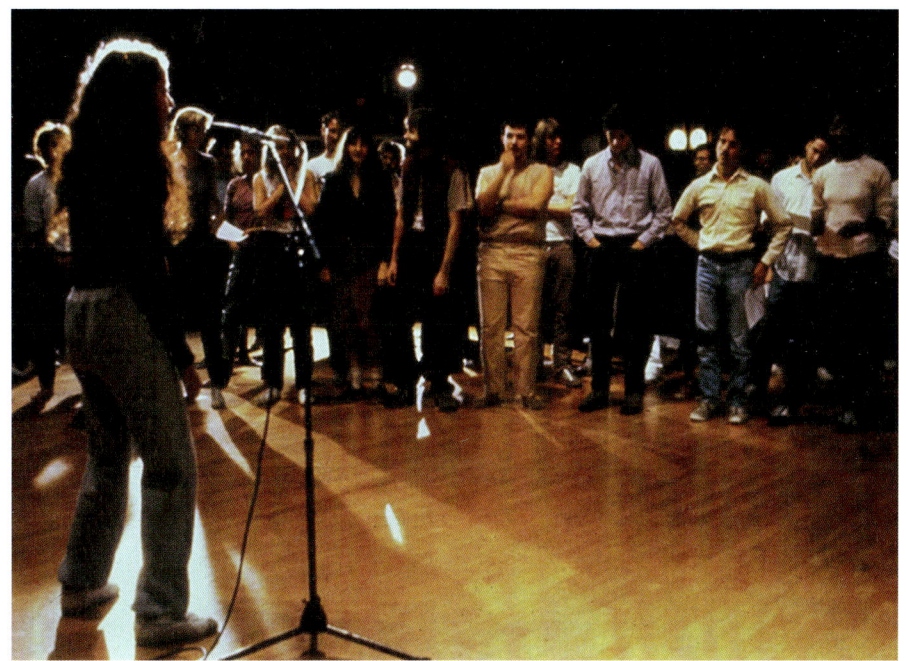

Adrian Piper
Funk Lessons 1983–4
Photograph documenting
the group performance,
University of California at
Berkeley, 1983

collective, shared, enjoyable experience'.[53] Piper's work,
like Boyce's, is uninterested in its collaborator-participants
achieving the competence and spectator-oriented
entertainment that Piper saw as underpinning social dance in
white culture; instead, both artists foster collective experiences
in which individuals develop expressive means alongside
other participants. Most of Boyce's recent performances have
invited participants to move closer, to listen and respond to
each other's movements and vocalisations and, in so doing,
to explore their selfhood and test their inherited and self-
imposed limits.

OVERLEAF
FEELING HER WAY 2022
Ten-channel ultra-HD video
installation with sound,
wallpapers and sculpture
Dimensions variable
Installation view at the 59th
International Art Exhibition –
La Biennale di Venezia, 2022
See also pp.88–9

FEELING HER WAY 2022 (pp.36–7) was commissioned for
the British Pavilion at the 59th Venice Biennale in 2022, for
which Boyce was awarded the Golden Lion prize for Best
National Participation. The work was conceived and produced
as the COVID-19 pandemic unfolded and the Black Lives Matter
movement resonated globally following the killing of George
Floyd. FEELING HER WAY took as a starting point (and included
elements of) the earlier *Devotional Collection*. Across different
galleries, moving-image works were presented on screens

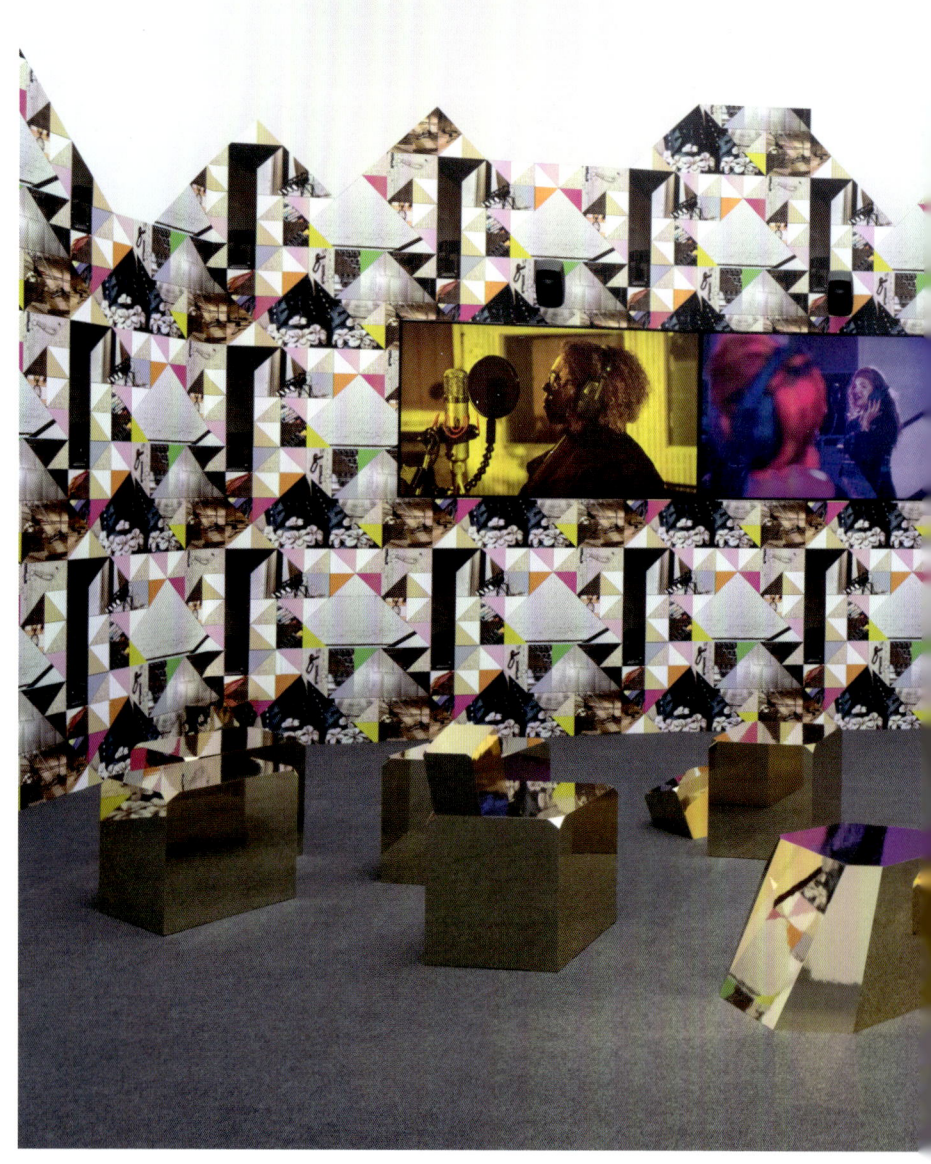

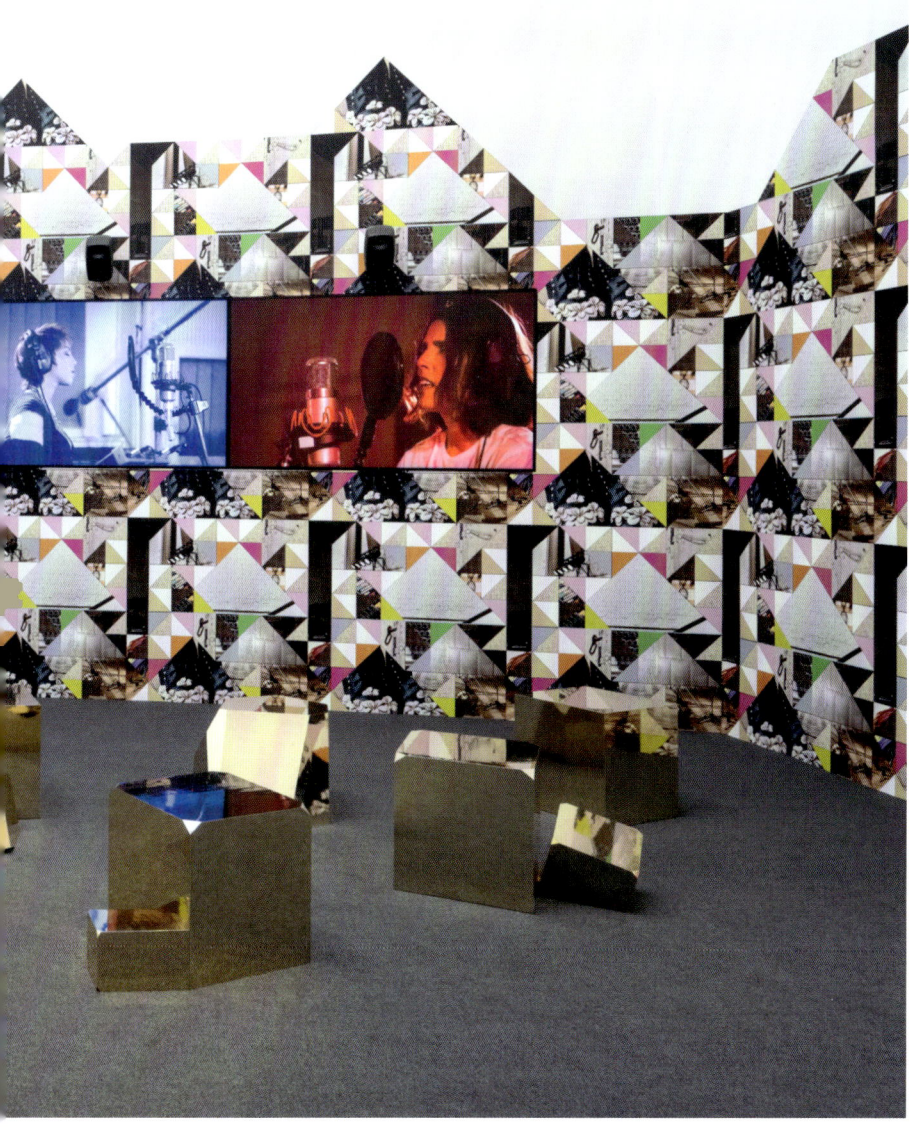

of different sizes, each showing edited sections of audio and video captured in recording studios. The performers we see and hear are professional lead singers Poppy Ajudha, Jacqui Dankworth, Sofia Jernberg and Tanita Tikaram, being led by composer Errollyn Wallen into different forms of improvisation and collaboration through instructions that invite the singers to play with and respond to each other's voices.

The installation features videos of solo performances, duets and collective singing, framed by kaleidoscopic, tessellating wallpaper designs collaging geometric patterns of different materials and textures. The footage of different singers is saturated in different hues – yellow, purple and red. Gold is another dominant colour, glowing on some of the wallpaper designs and covering the seating designed by the artist. Resembling a conglomeration of cubic crystals of pyrite, the seating both enhances a sense of artifice and resonates with the polyrhythms of jazz – a shared influence among the singers. Similarly, Boyce's method in combining fragments of images in her wallpapers has a clear relationship to the process of editing footage filmed with various cameras and then showing it across multiple screens in different spatial configurations. Collage remains a guiding principle: an activity that combines disparate fragments into an encounter and conversation that eschews linearity and continuity in favour of multiplicity, openness and spontaneity.

Across four adjacent monitors that form one part of FEELING HER WAY, three vocalists' joint improvisations are interspersed with Wallen's requests and responses. Wallen praises the singers, reminding them, too: 'Don't try and think about making a good sound.' The vulnerability of professional singers asked to let go of the external and internal expectations to achieve beautiful sounds is, at times, palpable; it is mirrored by the discomfort that many visitors – myself among them – undoubtedly felt at being challenged to listen in a new way and to a different purpose. This particular session reaches a climax when Wallen calls out one last prompt, the only one involving an assertion and an arresting one: 'I am a queen.' The statement sparks the exhilarating interplay of a striking range of performances. Following the recording, Ajudha remarked: 'We're singing in a way we haven't sung before. We're negotiating the space in ways we haven't done before.'[54]

In FEELING HER WAY, as in much of Sonia Boyce's recent work, the fear and shame that might otherwise be associated with failing to meet expectations gives way to a mutual process in which the participants dig deeper into their self and push their internal barriers. They do so by exploring the creative potential of formlessness and spurring one another to imagine unexpected forms of play and interaction, dissolving notions of stable order and harmonic continuity in favour of the expression of vitality as an act and state of becoming. This process reflects the uncompromising stance of an artist unafraid to play against set expectations about how art should behave and to make work that is simultaneously self-aware, visceral and open-ended.

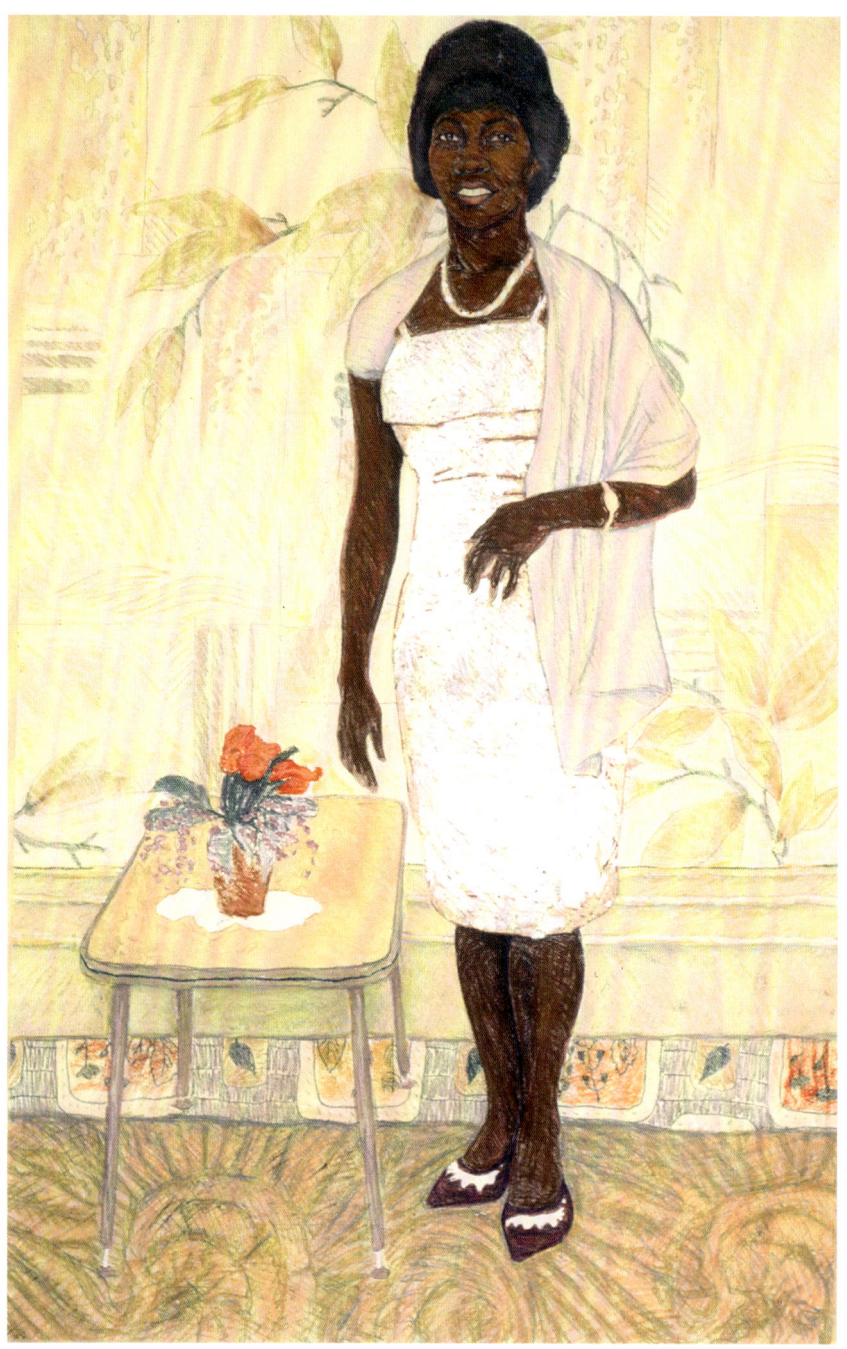

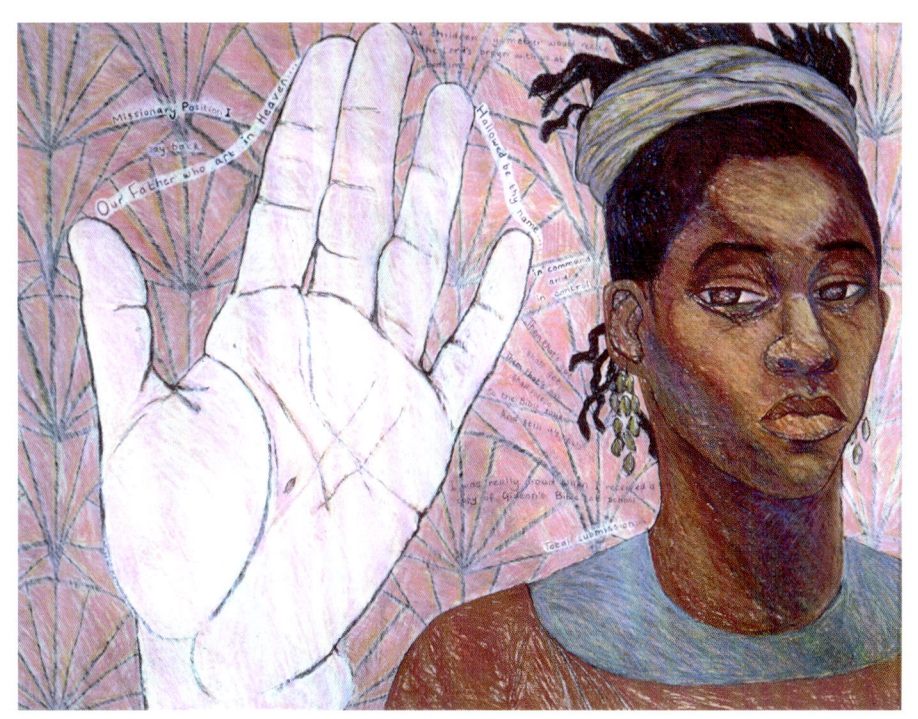

Auntie Enid – The Pose 1985
Gouache, pastel and
crayon on paper
183 × 123

*Missionary Position I – Lay
Back* 1985
Pastel on paper
77.5 × 103

OVERLEAF
Missionary Position II 1985
Watercolour, pastel and
crayon on paper
123.8 × 183

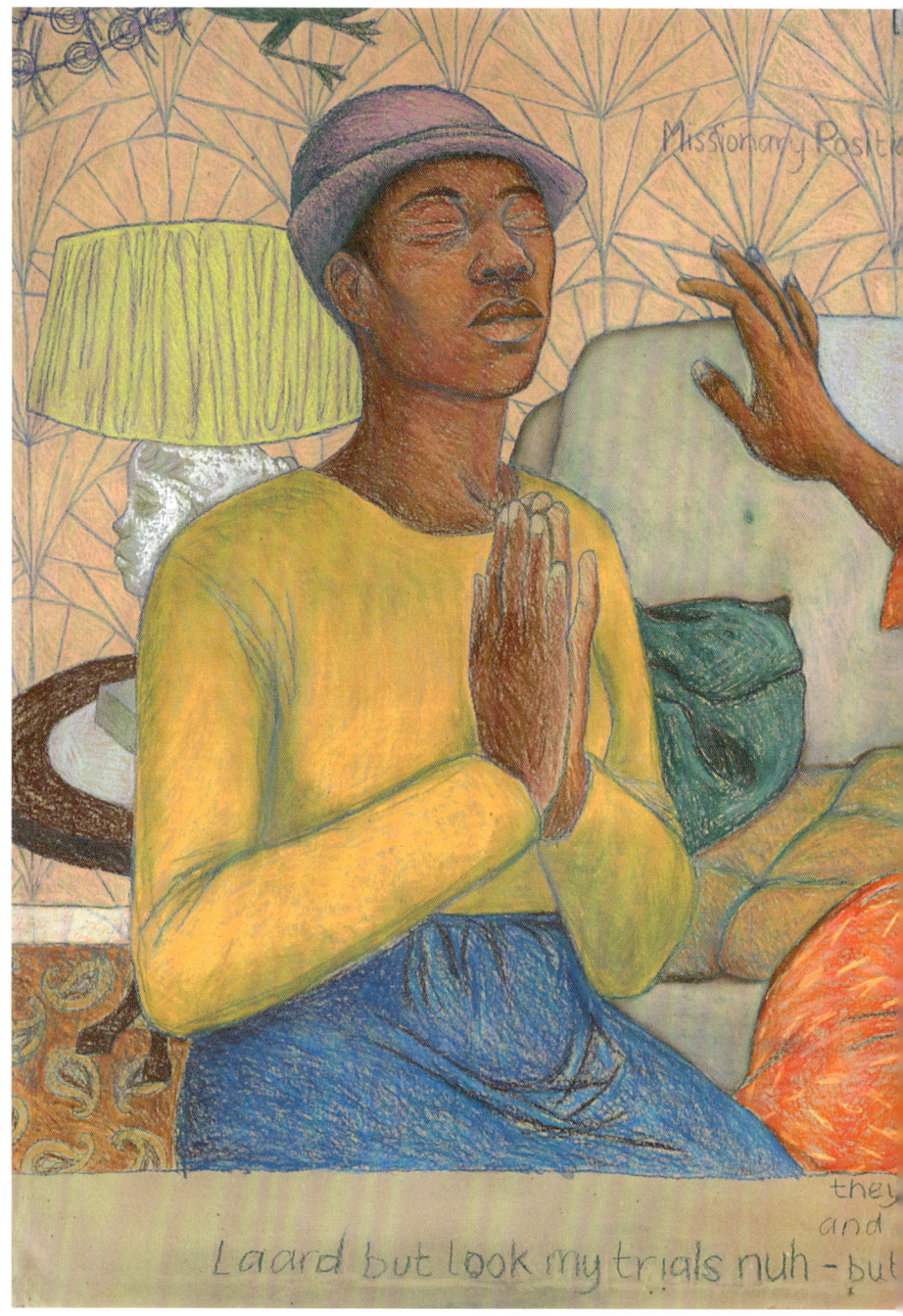

Missionary Rosita

they
and
Laard but look my trials nuh - but

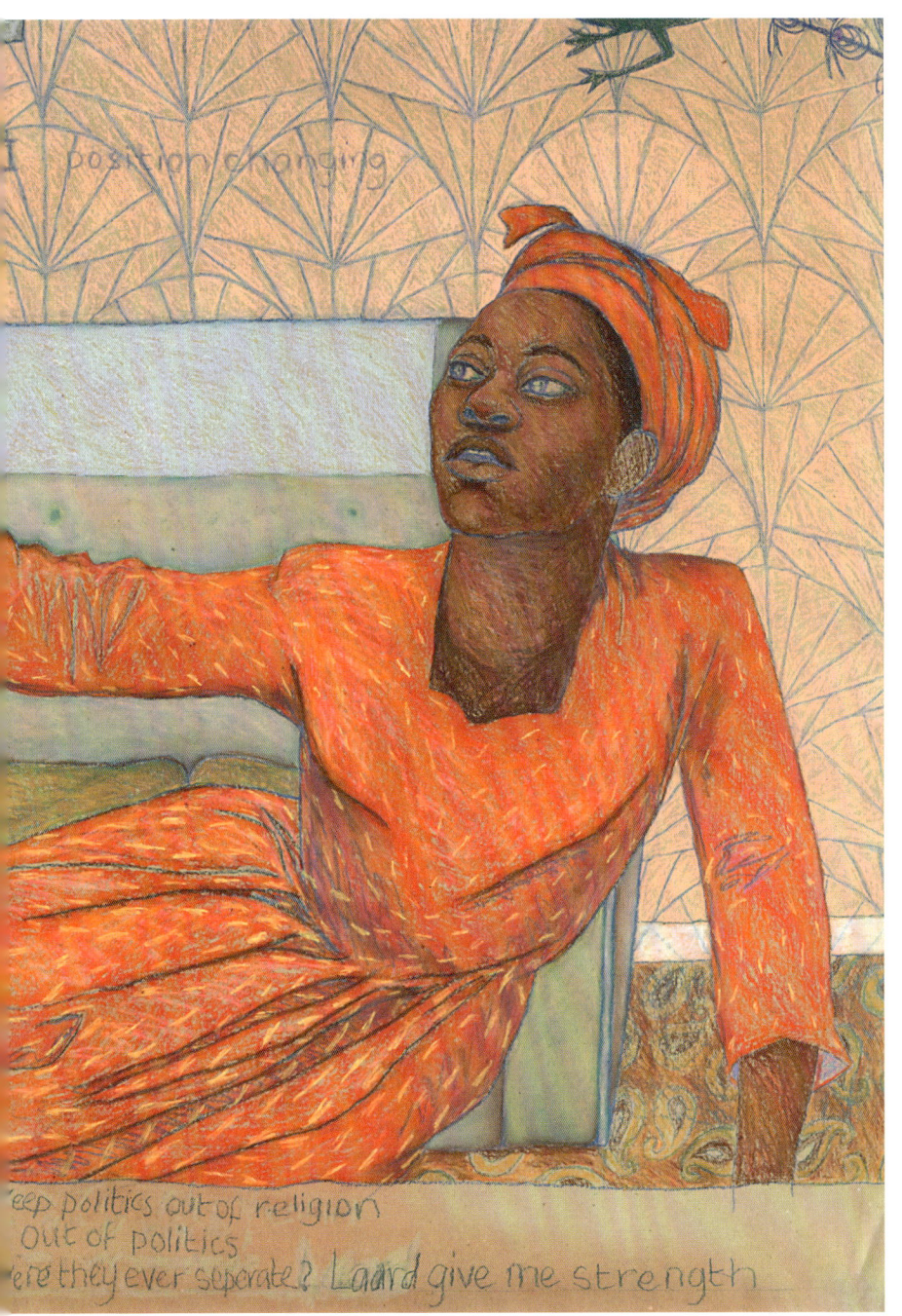

I position changing

eep politics out of religion
out of politics
ere they ever seperate? Laard give me strength

43

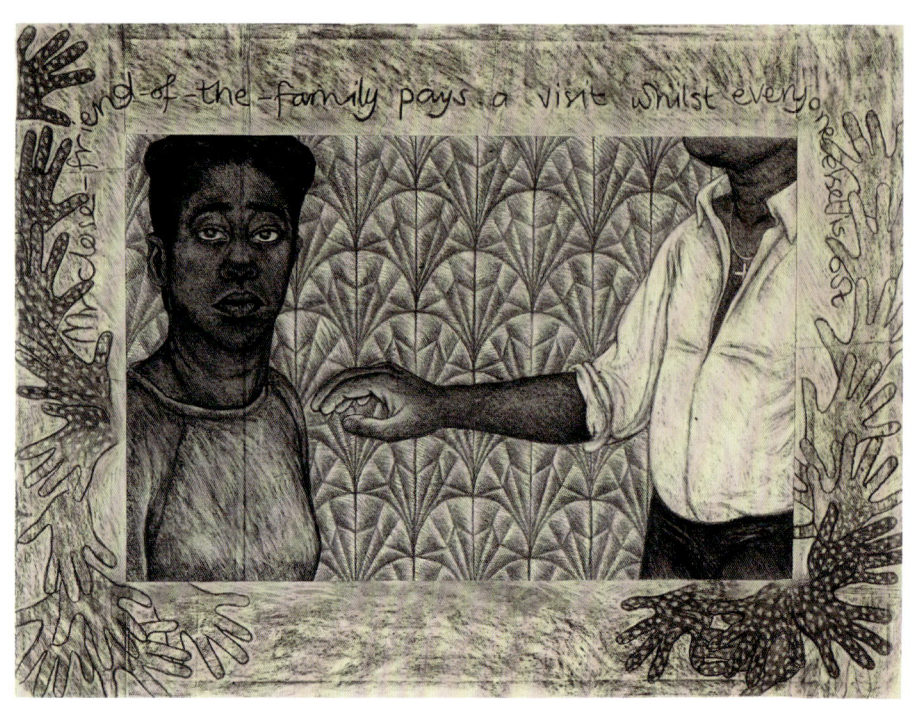

Mr-Close-Friend-of-the-Family
Pays a Visit Whilst Everyone
Else is Out 1985
Charcoal on paper
109.2 × 150

*She Ain't Holding Them
Up, She's Holding On
(Some English Rose)* 1986
Oil pastel and pastel on
paper
227 × 113.5

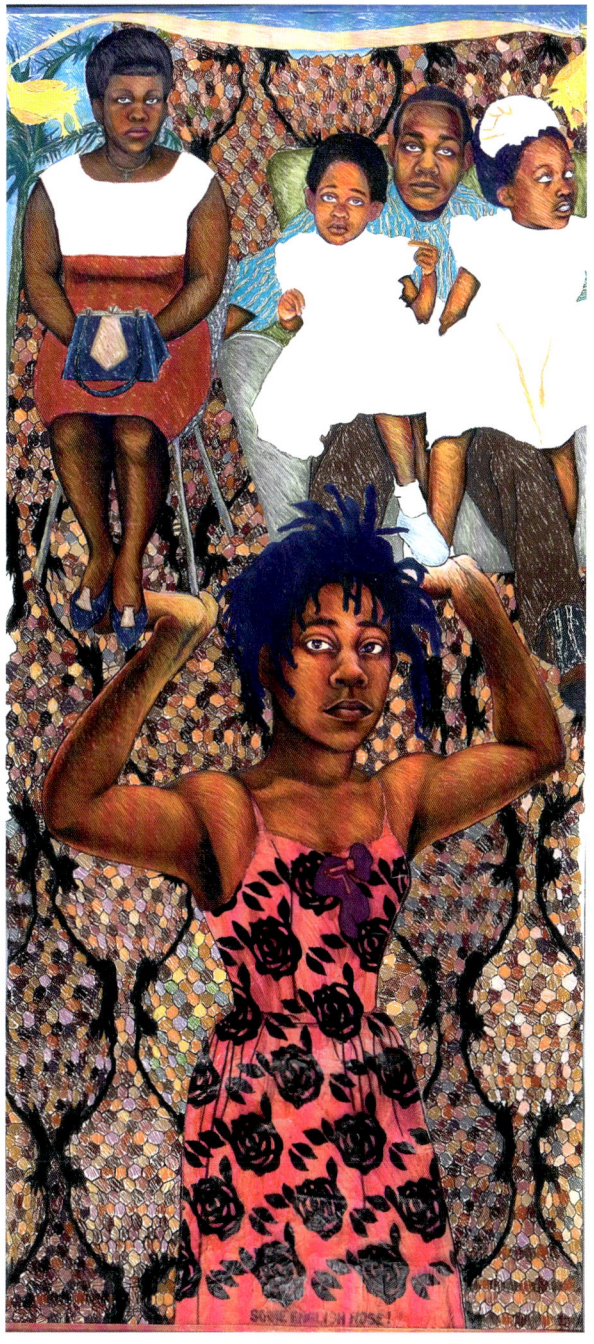

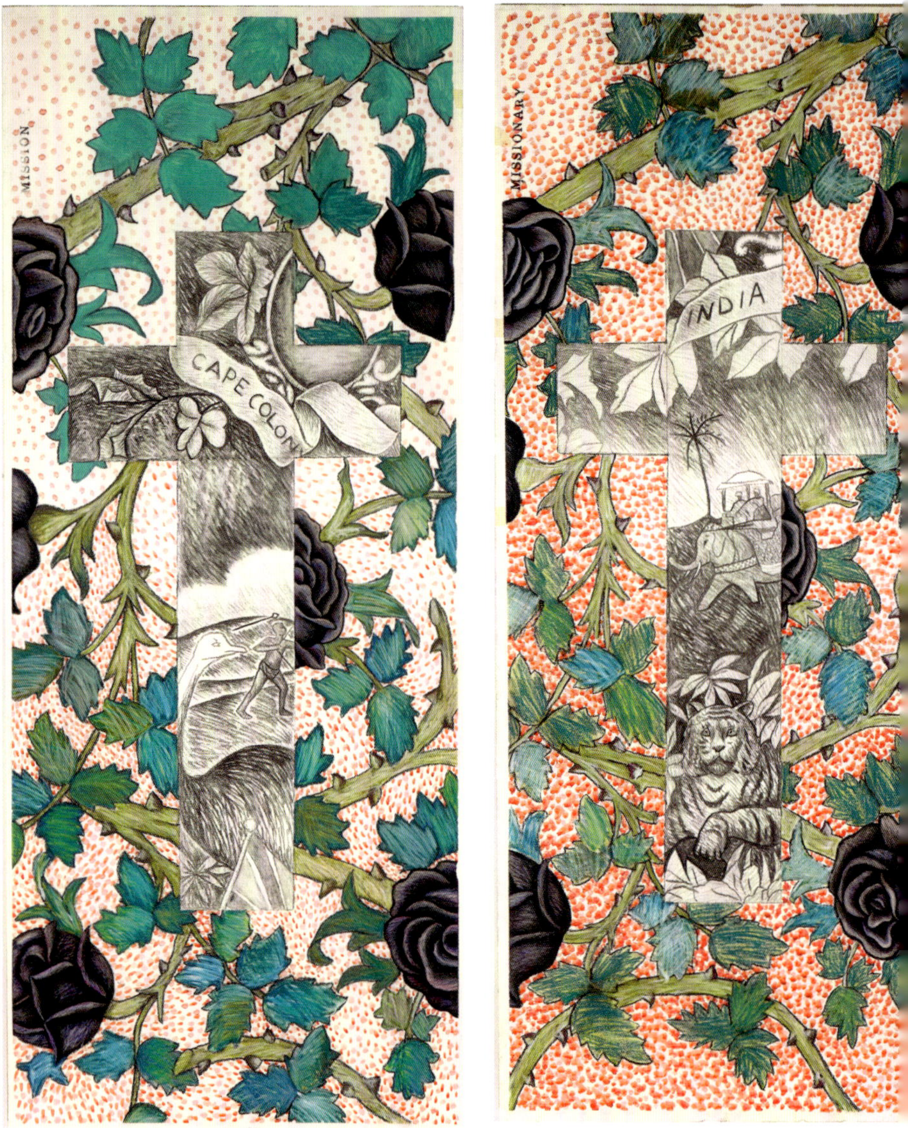

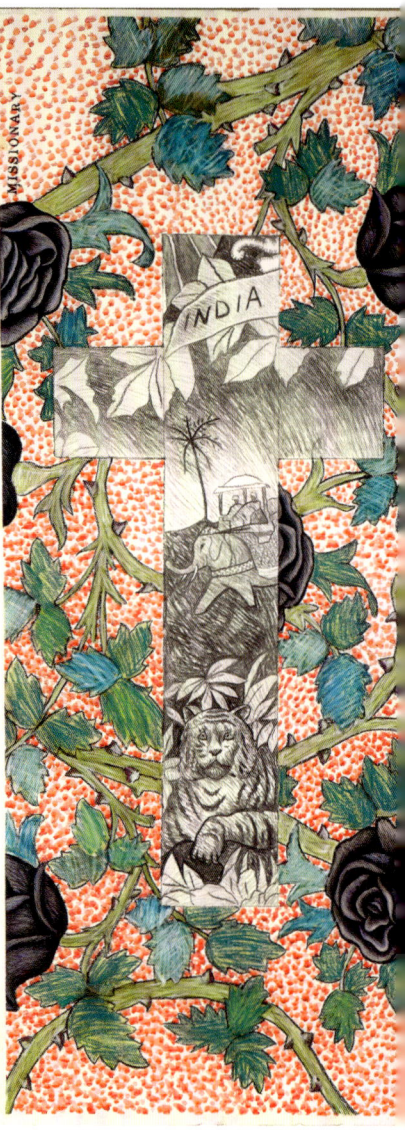

Lay Back, Keep Quiet and
Think of What Made Britain
So Great 1986
Charcoal, pastel and
watercolour on paper
Four parts, each 152.5 × 65

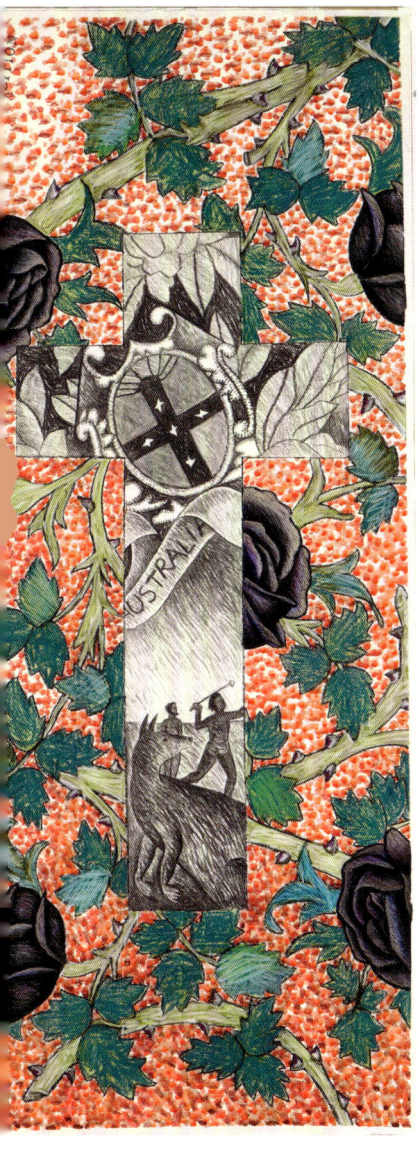

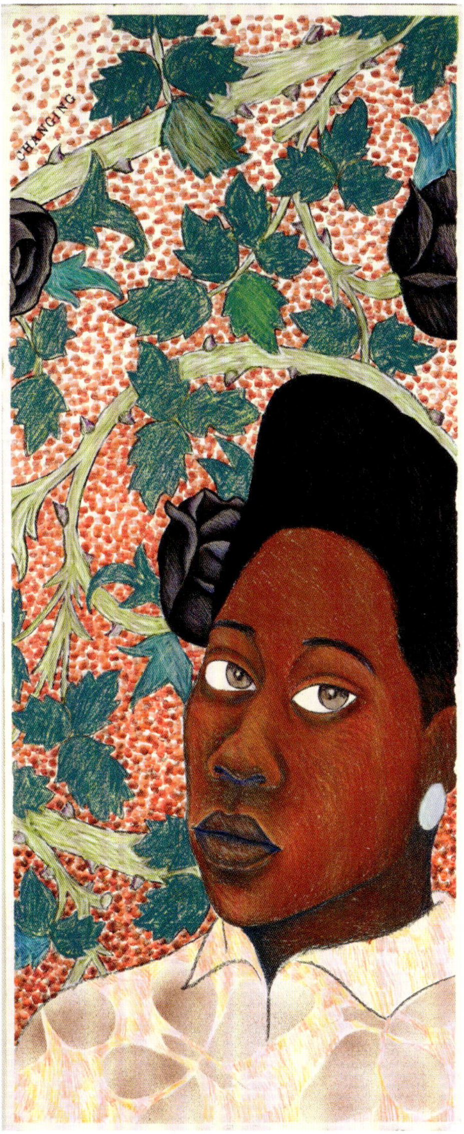

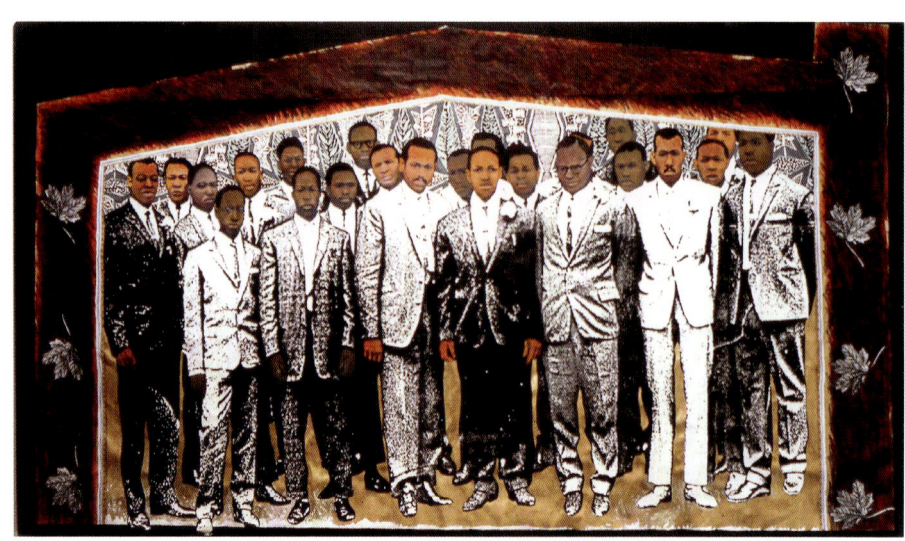

*Cricket Days Domino Nights
young arrivals/new home/
homeless. The streets are paved
with gold in the green and
pleasant land 1986*
Pastel and mixed-media
on collaged photographs
120 × 300

*From Someone Else's Fear
Fantasy to Metamorphosis*
1987
Acrylic paint, ink and
felt-tip pen on collaged
photographs
120 × 80

OVERLEAF
Talking Presence 1988
Pastel on paper on collaged
photographs with acrylic
paint
183 × 123

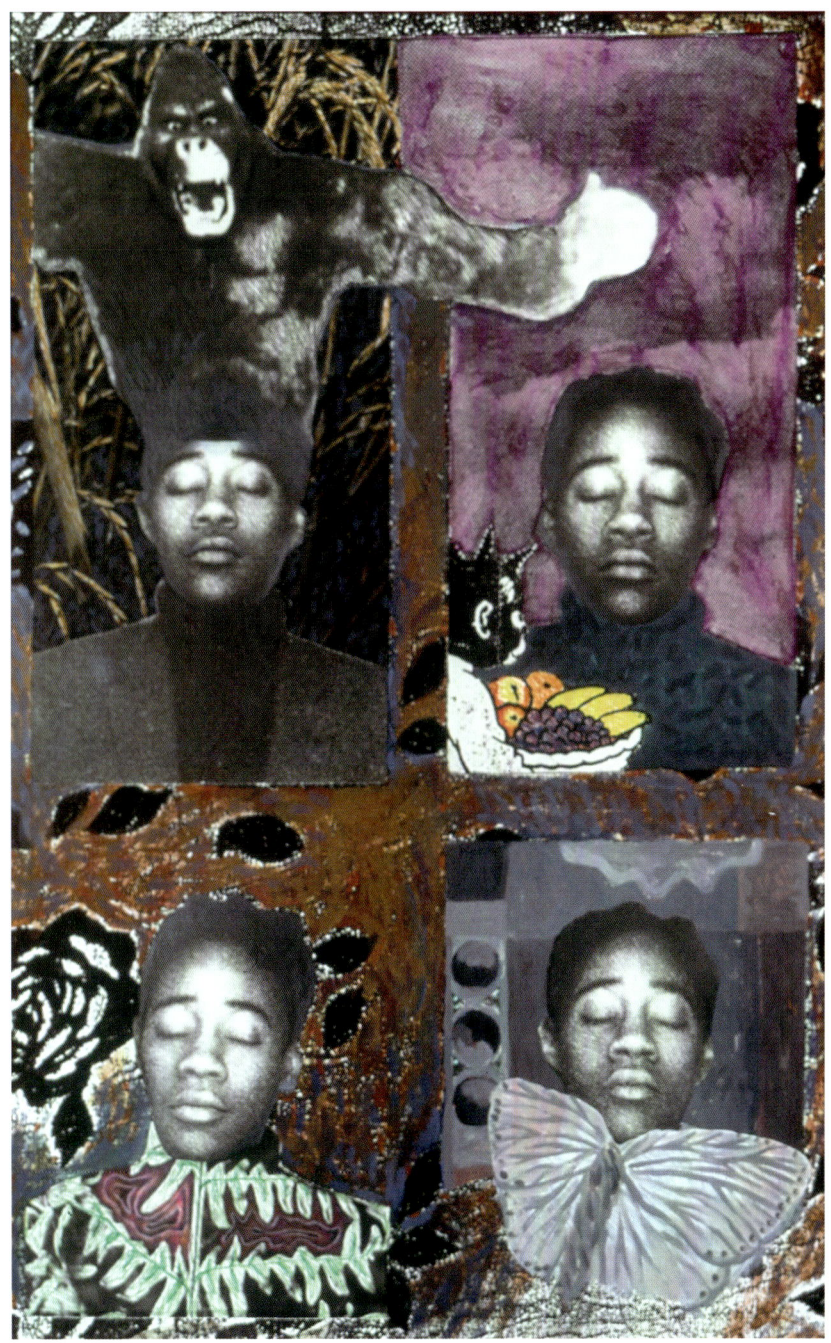

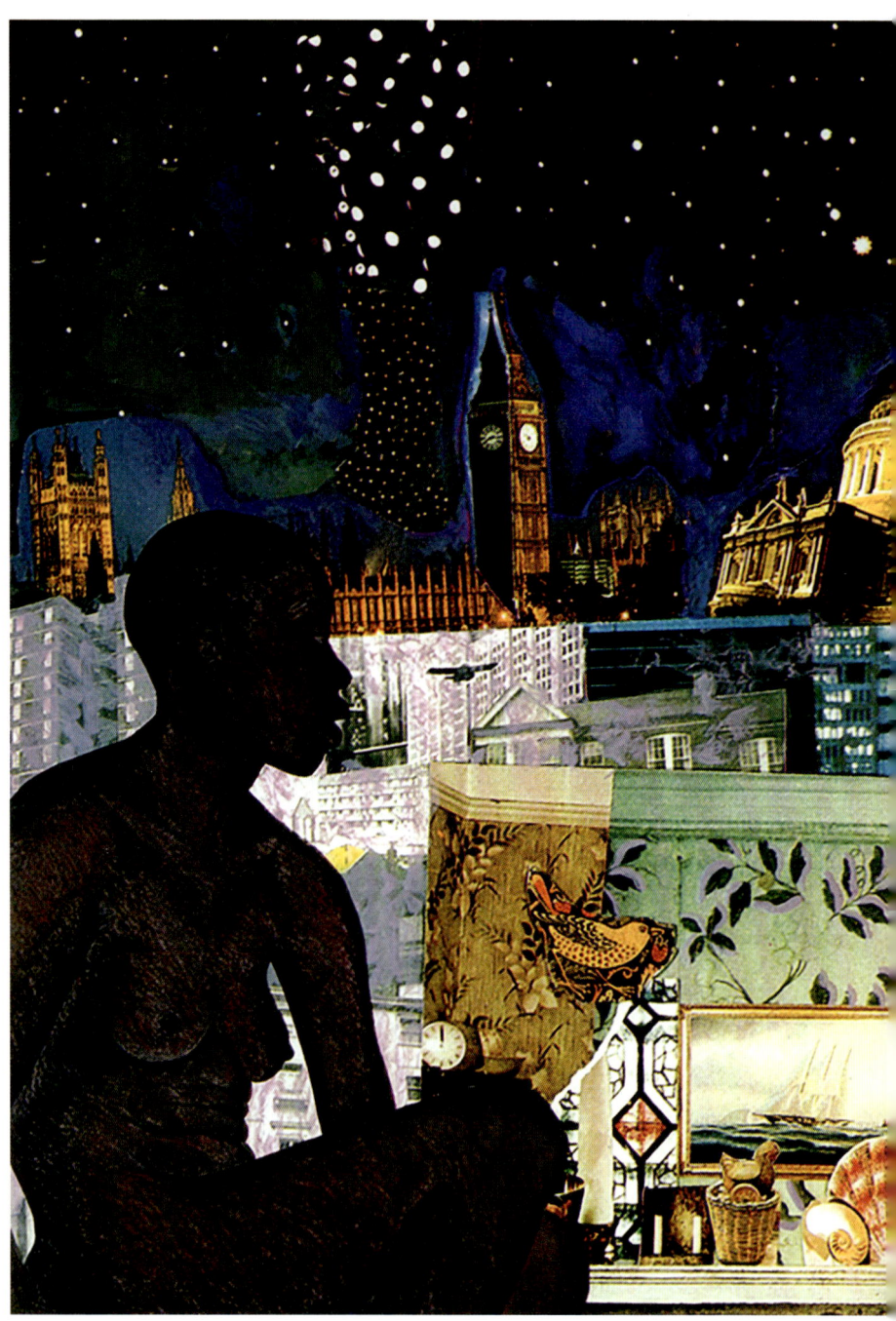

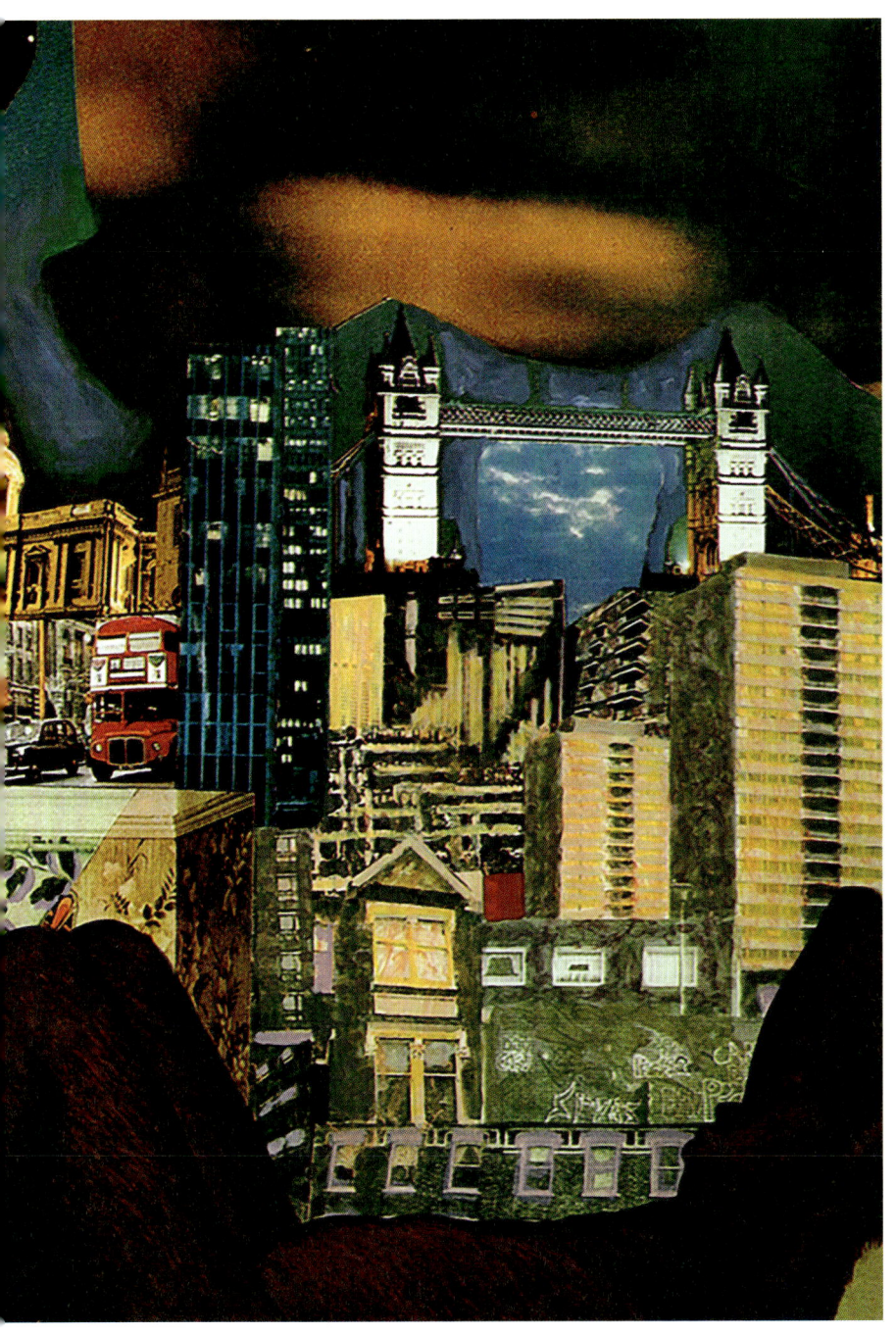

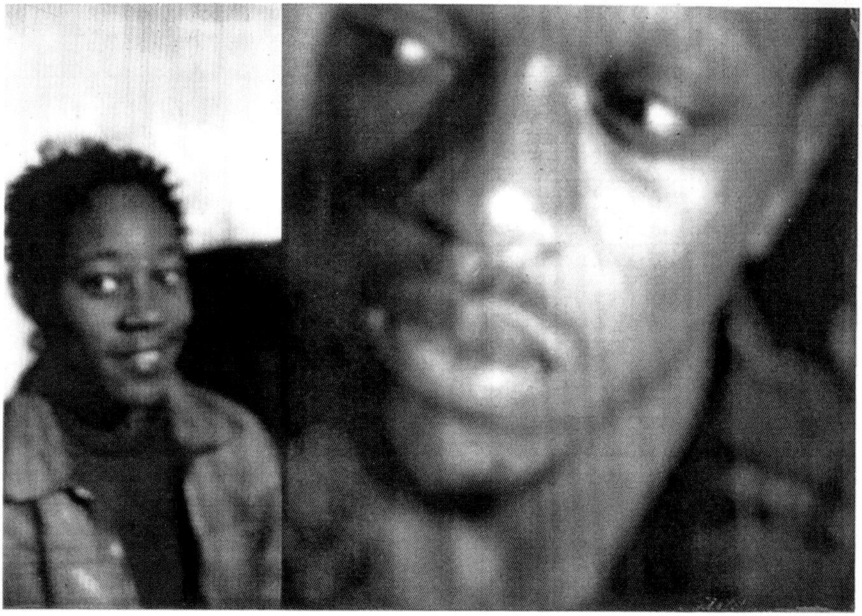

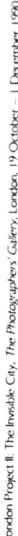

My dearest,

*It's summer at last, and what a scorcher. Everybody's
parading and grasping the sun or the warm night air.*

*Looking quite butch, I masquerade down Colville
Terrace on my way to Powis Square. That's when we
met. Actually less of a meeting more a moment.*

*Mesmerised by the dampness shimmering in the
parting of his lips. Get up uh ooh baby. Magnetic
moments shiver your bone and catch the smile in my
eyes.*

*What a feeling. Everyone's out today. Sliding to the
rift of the beat. Amidst the dull bustling humidity.
Bump to the rhumba. Pump and bubble down. Don't
look now you're being watched and face imminent
barricades.*

Catch you later,

Sonia Boyce, Carnival, 3 October 1990

London Project II: The Invisible City, The Photographers' Gallery, London, 19 October – 1 December 1990

The Ticket Machine 1990
2 of 6 printed postcards
(front and back) with text
Dimensions variable

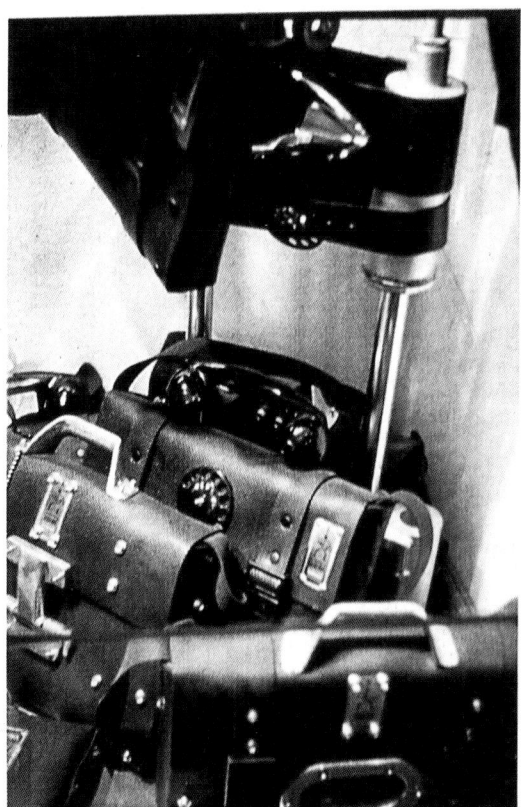

My dearest,

The wait at the bus stop can take a while. Twenty minutes maybe. Ask the conductor to put you off at the petrol station. The house is directly opposite. Try to get there for 8pm.

When you get there the conversation will be warm and familiar. Someone will clear their throat. Then the business will begin.

The agenda is drawn and quartered: funding bodies; rotating chair; NALGO reps; paper sales; anti-everything demos; mortgage repayments; notification from the bank (pause for laughter); the bailiffs; special items; no smoking; fitness plans; workaholics anonymous; relationships versus celibacy; hidden agendas; devisive strategies; any other business; digestives and tea all round.

Mary and Ann-Marie will slip away half way through the evening. They always do. The rest of us will shift and curl up on the bed, sofa and floor.

In the morning we'll wake up with Kiss FM, back aches, sore throats and stiff necks.

In sisterhood.

Sonia Boyce, Management Committee, 3 October 1990

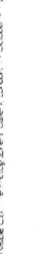

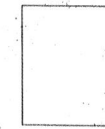

AM A SHY 19-year-old who is ... for a young man to spend my life with. He ... st be 5'8" or over very romantic and well ... ed. My interests include music, reading, ... out and anything interesting. pit pen to ... ... if you think you can brighten up my life ... old essential in hrs. we will please. Lon ... n area.
7789

A JAMAICAN MALE/STUD 24 wishes to meet ... and around 6ft tall work ... aged 24 upwards for soc ... with a religious ... back ... good laugh. Replies from ... ween 25 and 33 ... s I enjoy ... ed but will consider oth ... ing and corresponding no dro ... smoker preferred. London ar ...
7783

AM AN ATTRACTIVE 34-year-old single ... other of Carib ... origin who enjoys music ... ... and good com ... ading the g ... like to correspond ... han ... ... than. I w ... ged between 30 and 40 years, ... tractive m ... an origin with a genuine and ... se of Car ... plies from someone ... ing in the ... ... other areas welcome. London ... ...
7761

SINGLE 35-YEAR-OLD Jam ... one grown up child wishes to ... a gentleman for friendship ... a Seventh Day Adventist Chr ... reading, sewing, cooking, ... crocheting include ... Jamaican. W.I.

R-OLD by girl who is sh ... ... grooves. I would ... boys of the same age. I ...
778

INGLE 28-YEAR-OLD Seventh Day Adven ... ... nal Afro-Caribbean origin. wishes to ... ... with a male of Caribbean origin ag ... 26 to 35 years and at least 5'7" tall with ... ... I am caring, nice and enjoy walks ... of the countryside, ... music. So on ... all. If you have similar interests get in touch ... Coventry area.
7782 CFF

A HARD WORKING 34 yea ... male aged 34 years and 5'8" t ... correspond with ... ween 24 and 36 ... s Jama ...

R-OLD black woman a ... a shy Taurean, al ... black theatre/dance. co ... ng etc. I would like to me ... ... taste and combe ... ... friendship and eve ... relationship. He must t ... ... ving understanding an ... t in touch if you are final ... aged between 28 an ... ... West Midland ... ... photo. Wes ...
7785

EMALE who 24 wishes to meet ... raight female aged 24 upwards for soc ... g and having a laugh. Replies from Lon ... on area ... but will consider others ... Middlesex area
7783

A GOOD LOOKING ... ... guy is in search of ... ... stable humorous sincere and ... guy. May be we can make ... ... ensures a r ... London area

AM A 34-YEAR-OLD pro ... male 5'9" tall ... ... to include visiting ... ... out and sport ... white ladies ages ... ... the London ... humour so ... ... London ...

VE 26 year old lady, ... I am caring, sincere, g ... dards and ambitions. ... ... versatile and a good life ... ... dern male of simila ... ... e and enjoy life. Phot ... but not essential. Lon ...
7785/L

I AM AN 18 y ... ... interesting and ... girl who is ... ... to help from home to grooves. I would ... ... the same age f ... don ar ...

I AM A VERY ATTRACTIV ... of West Indian ... ... and of average build. My in ... ... ing, parties, festiv ... ... by only Dru ... ... develop ... ... single gu ... ... serious friends ... ... share similar interests ... preferred London area.

VE white female wo ... ... eatre nature and ... ... tive, professional ... ... Pisces aged 35 plus ... with Photo and ph ... London area preferred

7777/VI

I AM A 26-YEAR-OLD black ... single parent. I'm a shy woman an ... overnight, loving, kind and loyal ... also ... include reggae music, black theatre, com ... ... dancing, reading etc. I would to meet ... a black man conscious ... and contented ... ready welcoming lasting relationship lead to ... ... a loving lasting relationship lead to ... intelligent, ambitious, loving, understanding and ... ... man woman Get in touch if you ... ...
Midlands area

SOUL ME AND ... black ... ... meet ... corresponds ...

D Arien black female w ... ... resting people from ar ... unlimited however tha ... ... conversation alway ... ... made Colour may ...

54

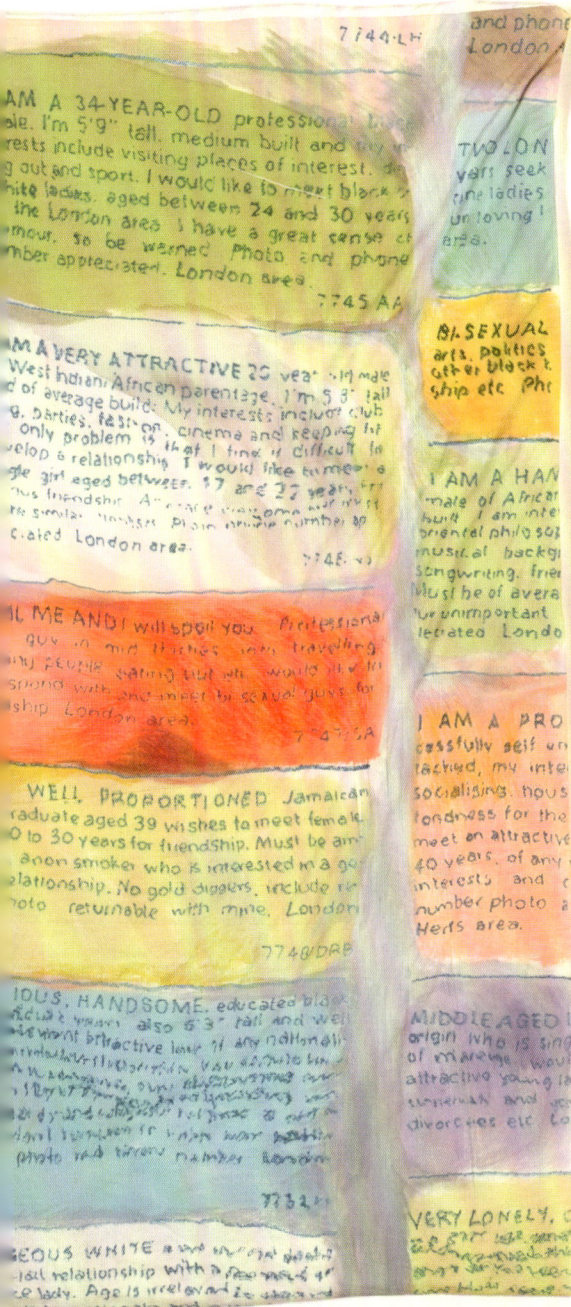

AM A 34-YEAR-OLD professional b...
...le. I'm 5'9" tall. medium built and ...
...rests include visiting places of interest. ...
...g out and sport. I would like to meet black ...
...hite ladies, aged between 24 and 30 years ...
...the London area. I have a great sense of ...
...mour. so be warned. Photo and phone ...
...mber appreciated. London area.

7745 AA ...

...M A VERY ATTRACTIVE 20 year old male ...
...West Indian/African parentage. I'm 5'3" tall ...
...d of average build. My interests include club ...
...g. parties. fashion, cinema and keeping fit ...
...only problem is that I find it difficult to ...
...velop a relationship. I would like to meet a ...
...gle girl aged between 17 and 27 years. fri ...
...hus friendship. A more important part ...
...re similar. Please phone number ap ...
...c.ated London area.

7746 ...

...L ME AND I will spoil you. Professional ...
...guy in mid thirties into travelling ...
...ny people. eating out etc. would like to ...
...spend with one other bisexual guys for ...
...ship. London area.

7747 ...

WELL PROPORTIONED Jamaican ...
...raduate aged 39 wishes to meet female ...
...0 to 30 years for friendship. Must be a n ...
...anon smoker who is interested in a go ...
...elationship. No gold diggers. include re ...
...hoto returnable with mine. London ...

7748/DAB ...

...IOUS, HANDSOME, educated black ...
...adult years. also 5'3" tall and well ...
...his want attractive lover if any nationali ...
...[illegible handwriting]...
...photo and phone number. London ...

7732 ...

...GEOUS WHITE ... ...
...ail relationship with a ... ...
...le lady. Age is irrelevant is ... ...

and phone
London ...

7744 LH

TWO LON ...
... years seek ...
...fine ladies ...
...un loving ...
...area.

BI-SEXUAL ...
...arts, politics ...
...other black ...
...ship etc. Pho ...

I AM A HAN ...
...male of African ...
...built. I am inte ...
...oriental philoso ...
...musical backgr ...
...songwriting. frie ...
...Must be of avera ...
...ur unimportant ...
...located Londo ...

I AM A PRO ...
...cessfully self em ...
...tached, my inte ...
...socialising. hous ...
...fondness for the ...
...meet an attractive ...
...40 years. of any ...
...interests and c ...
...number photo a ...
...Herts area.

MIDDLE AGED ...
...origin who is sing ...
...of mature ...
...attractive young la ...
...summerish and ...
...divorcees etc. Lo ...

VERY LONELY, co ...
...&...

Pillowcase 1990
Fabric dye, pen and crayon
on cotton
200 × 200

The Comforter 1993
Braided and sewn hair
26 × 17 × 12

Drawing from sketchbook 1986
Pastel on paper
21 × 14.9

Plaited and Knotted 1995
Braided hair
17 × 14 × 4

*Plaited and Sewn with Red
Satin Belly* 1993
Hair and satin
45.5 × 26.5 × 4

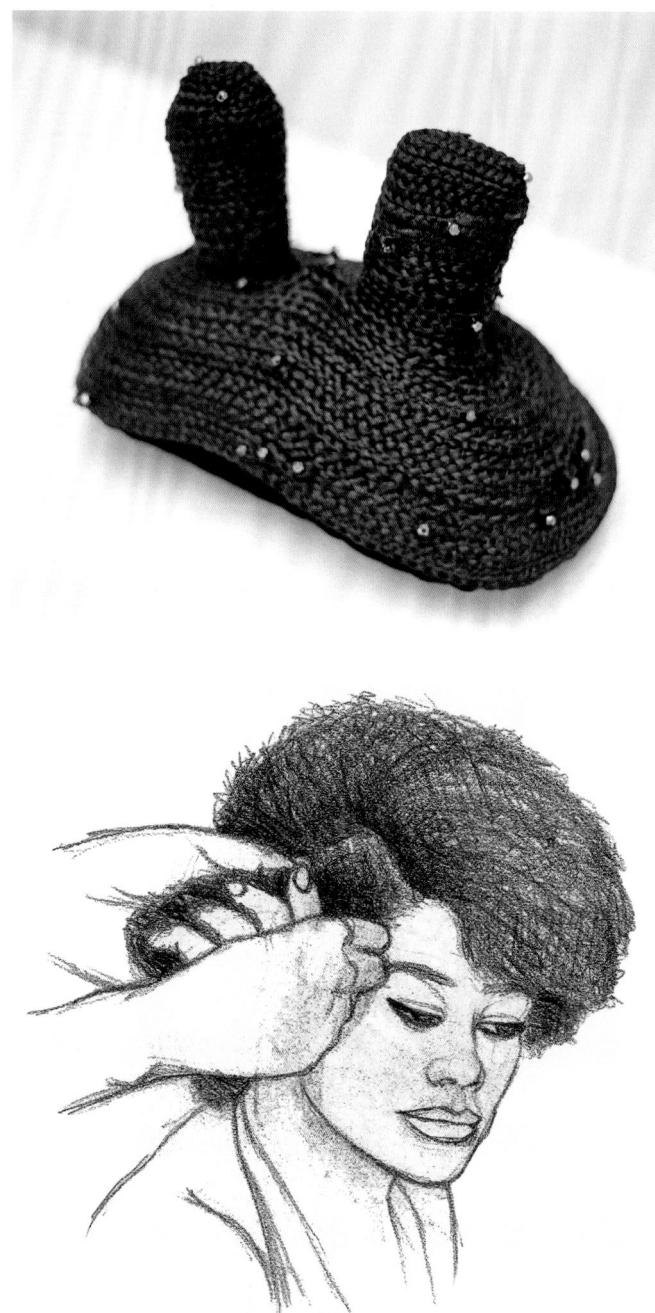

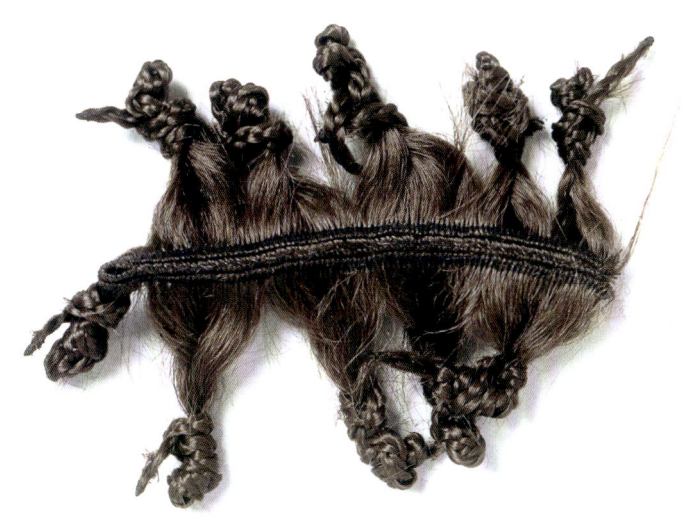

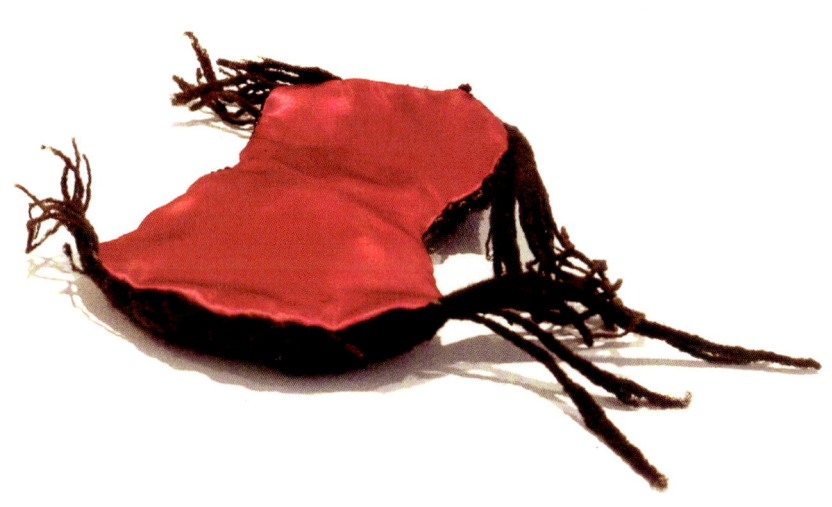

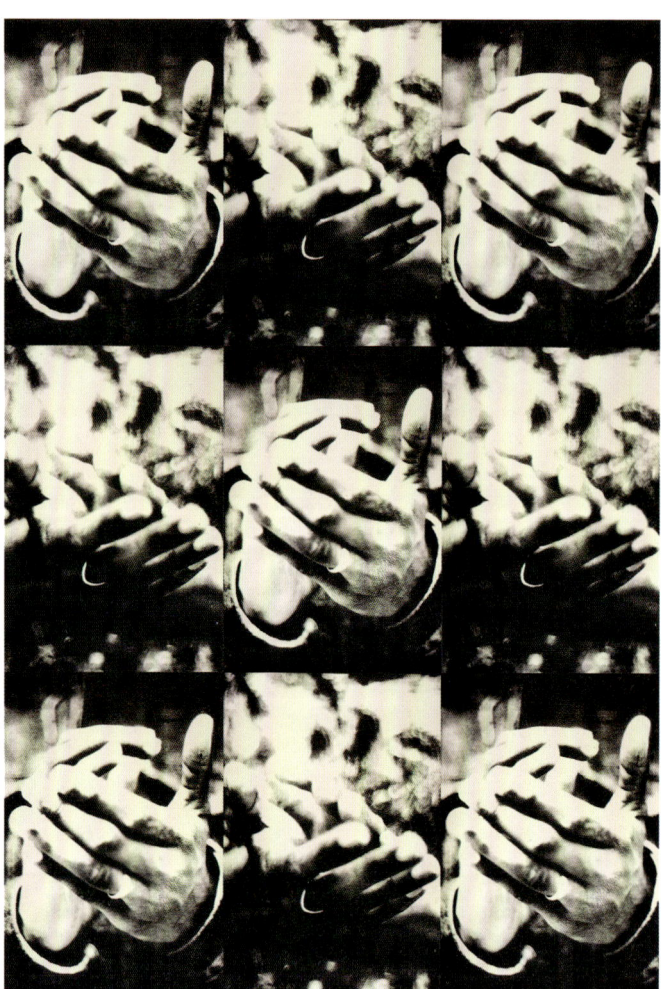

Clapping Wallpaper 1994
Screenprint on wallpaper
Dimensions variable

Afro Blanket 1994
37 Afro wigs
Dimensions variable
Installation view from
Wish You Were Here,
BANKSPACE, London
1994

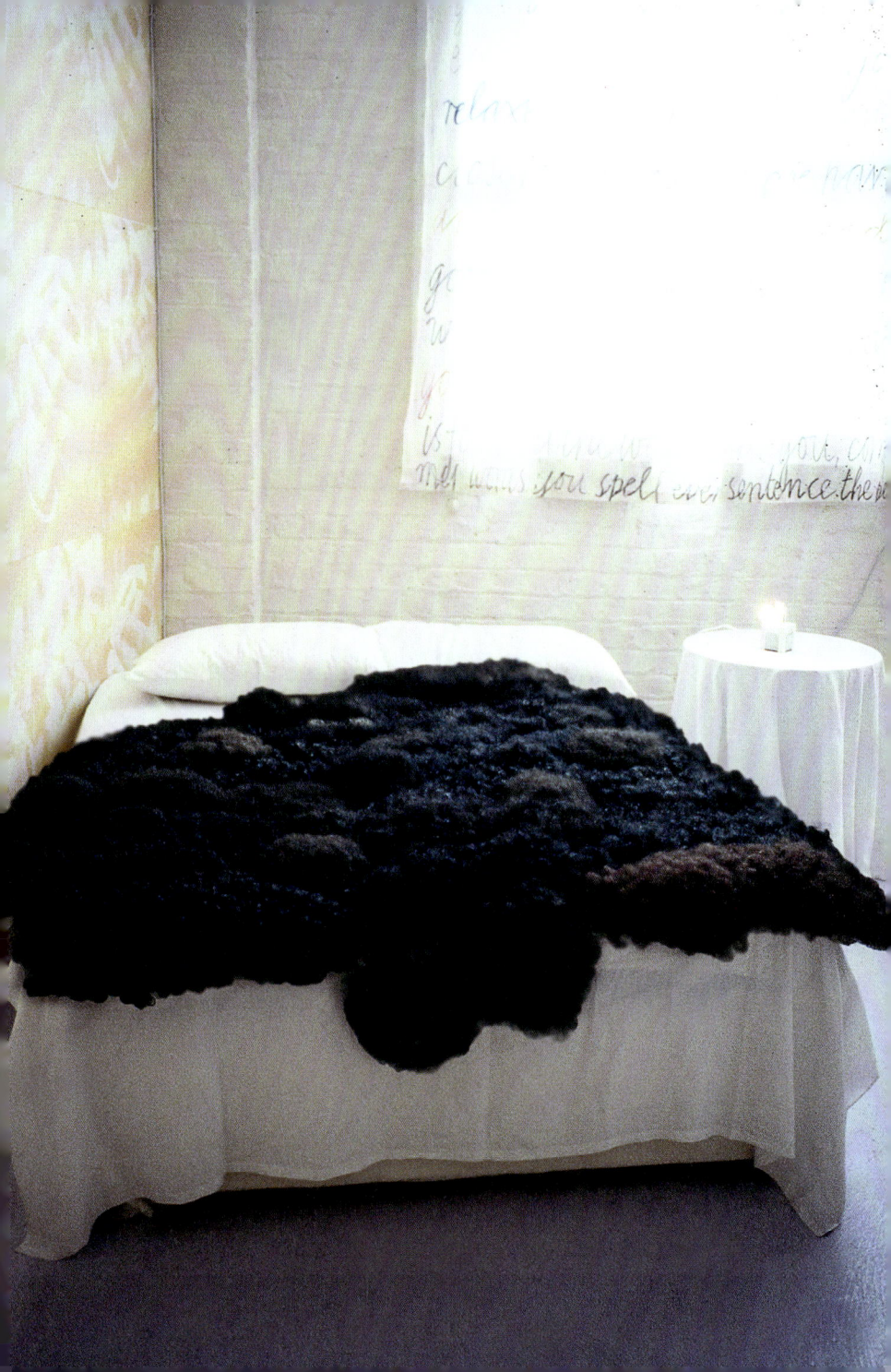

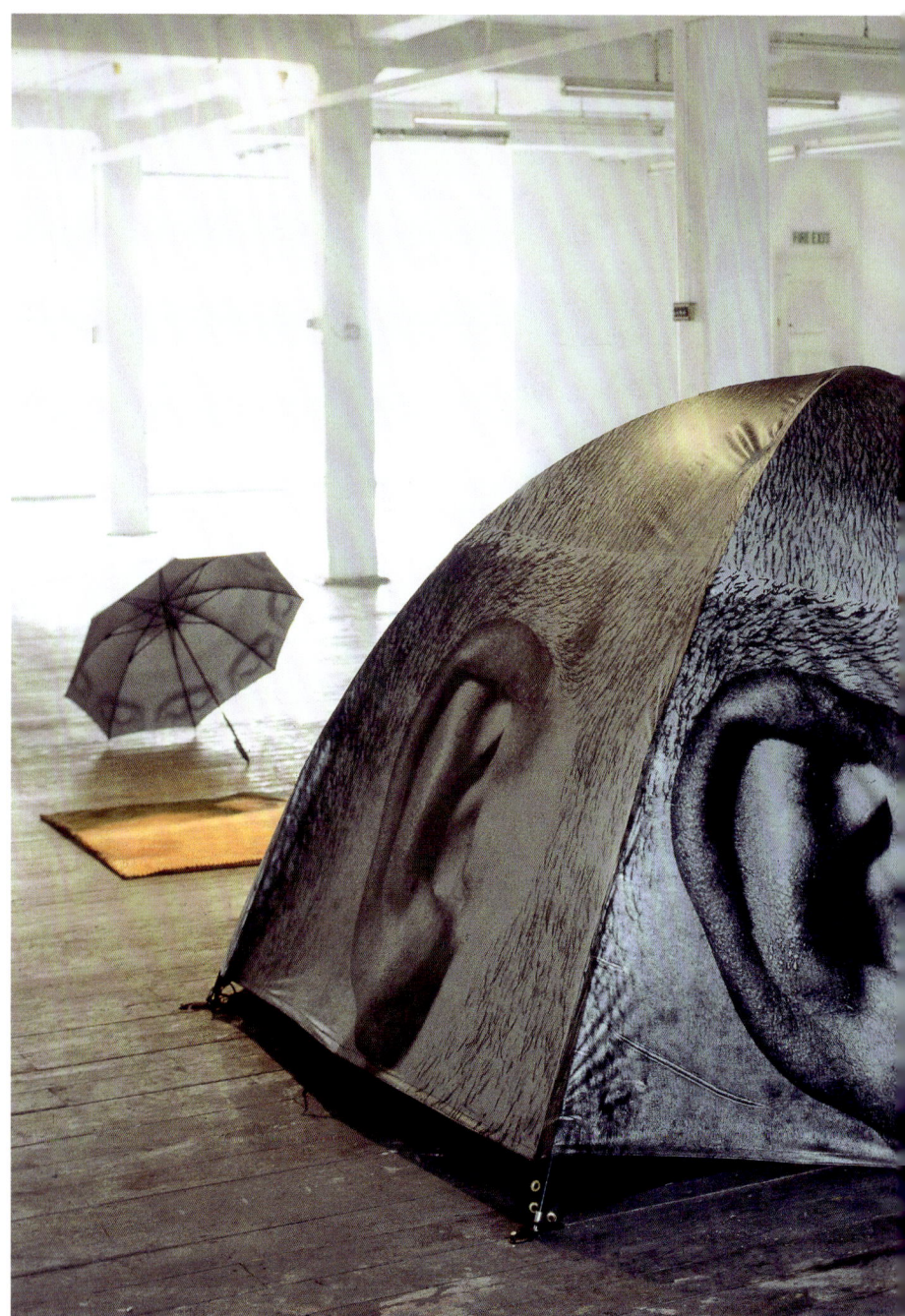

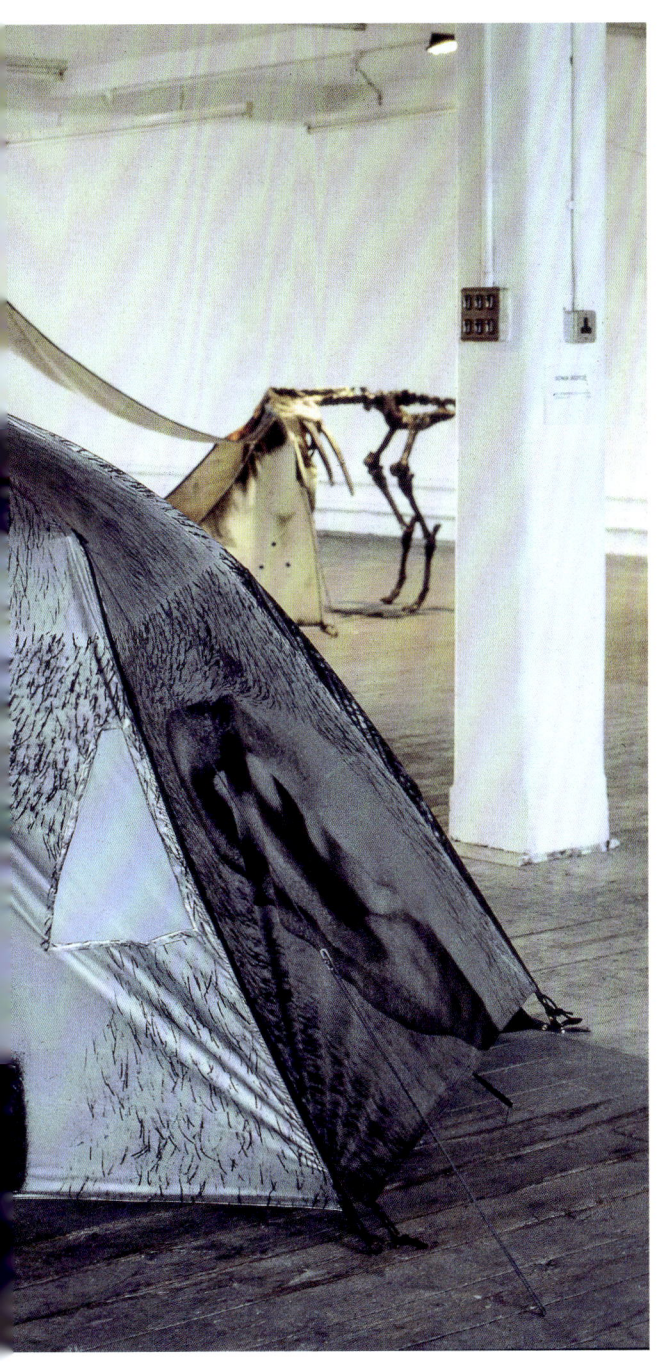

*Tent, Blanket and Umbrella –
The Beginnings of an Urban
Survival Kit* 1995
Tent (foreground), blanket
and umbrella (background)
Photo-silkscreen print on
tent, fabric and umbrella
Installation view, *Portable
Fabric Shelters*, London
Printworks Trust, London,
1995

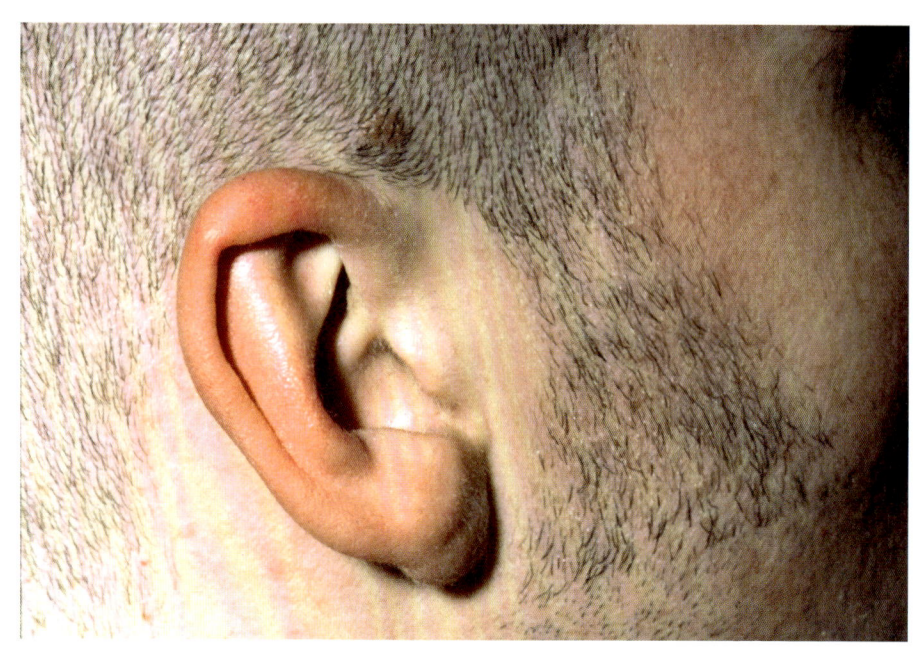

Head I (Skin) 1995
Full-colour blue-back
billboard print
91.5 × 137.5

Head II (Dread) 1995
Full-colour blue-back
billboard print
137.5 × 91.5

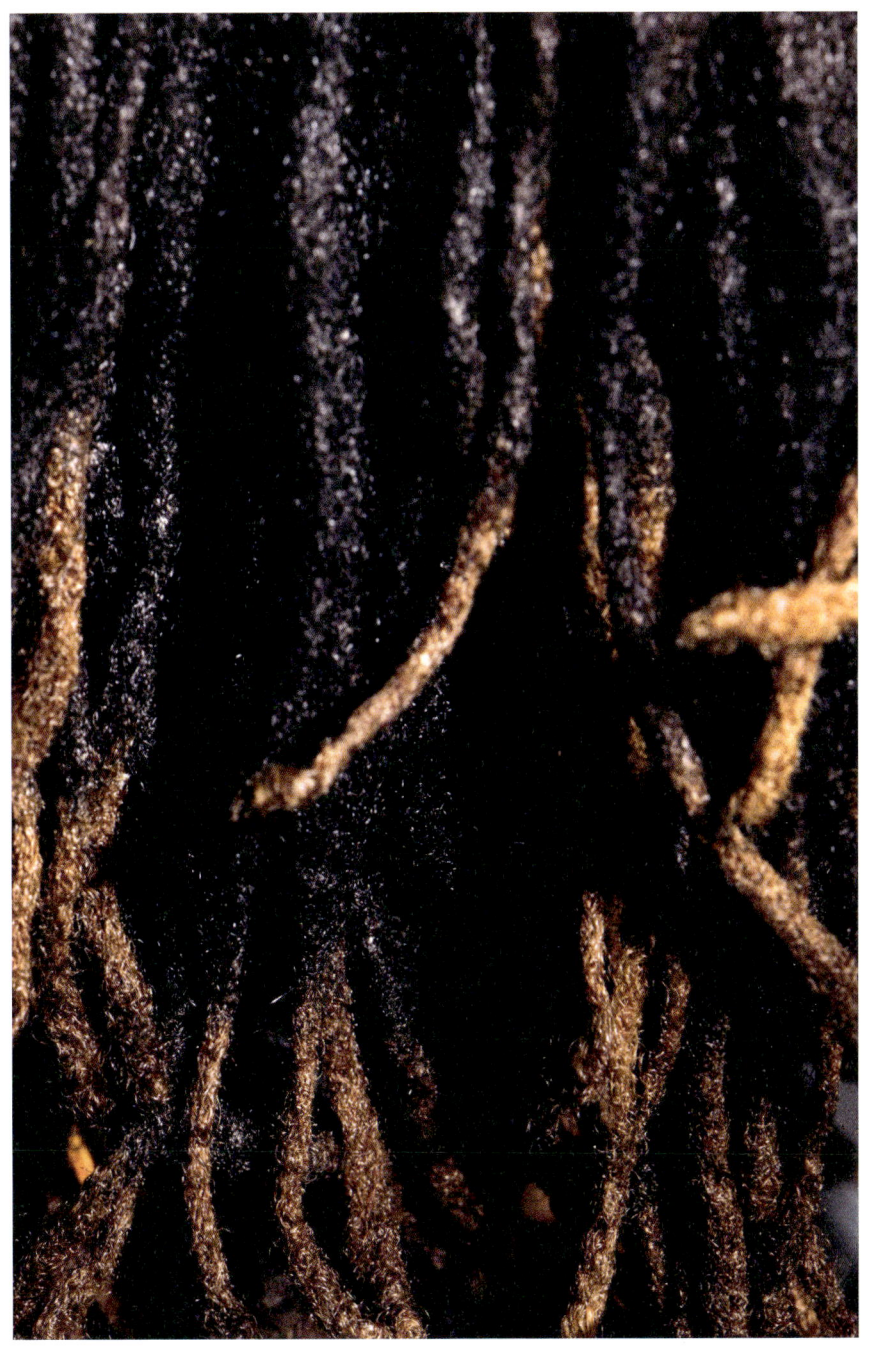

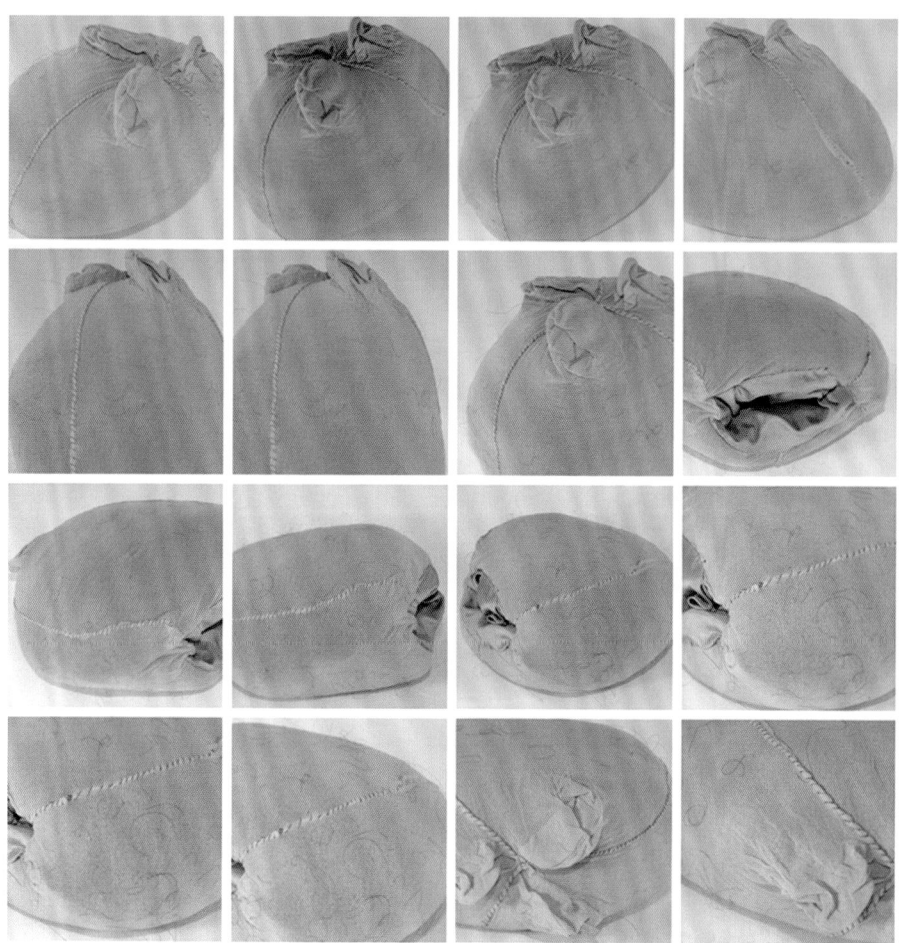

*Three Legs of Tights Stuffed
with Afro Hair* 1994, printed
2015
Photographic print on
aluminium
80 × 80

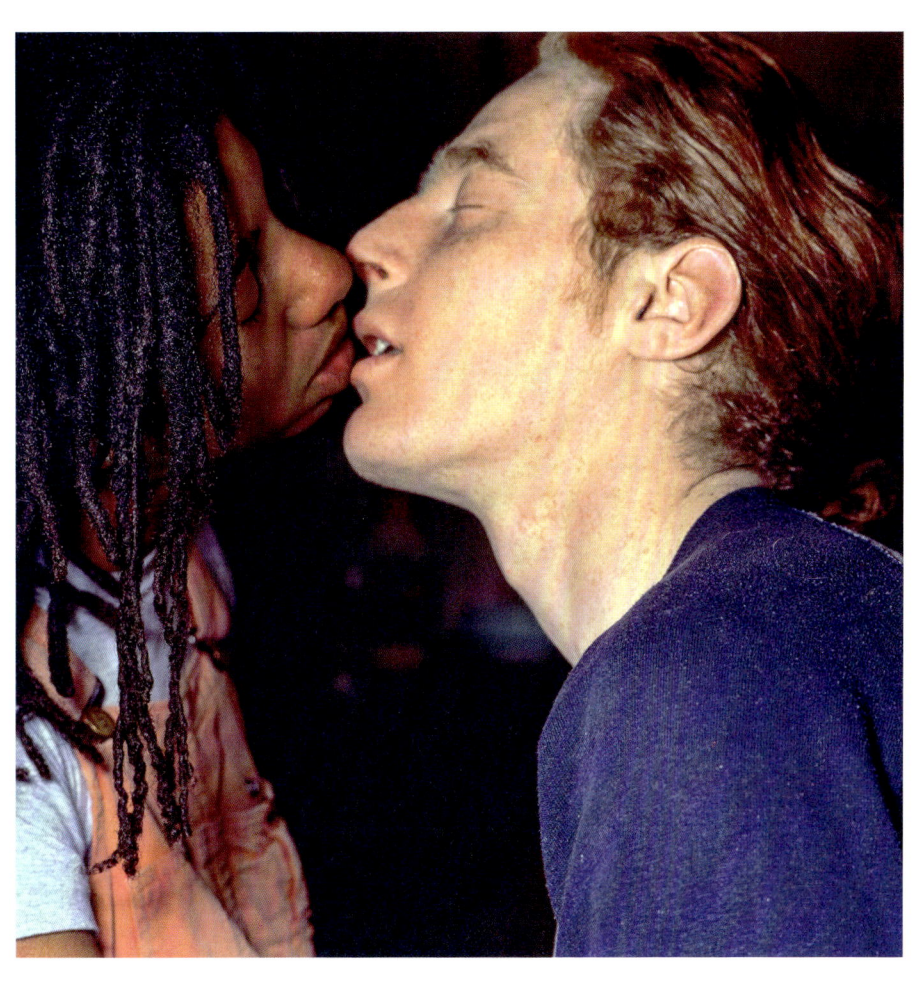

Untitled (Kiss) 1995
Photographic print on vinyl
300 × 300

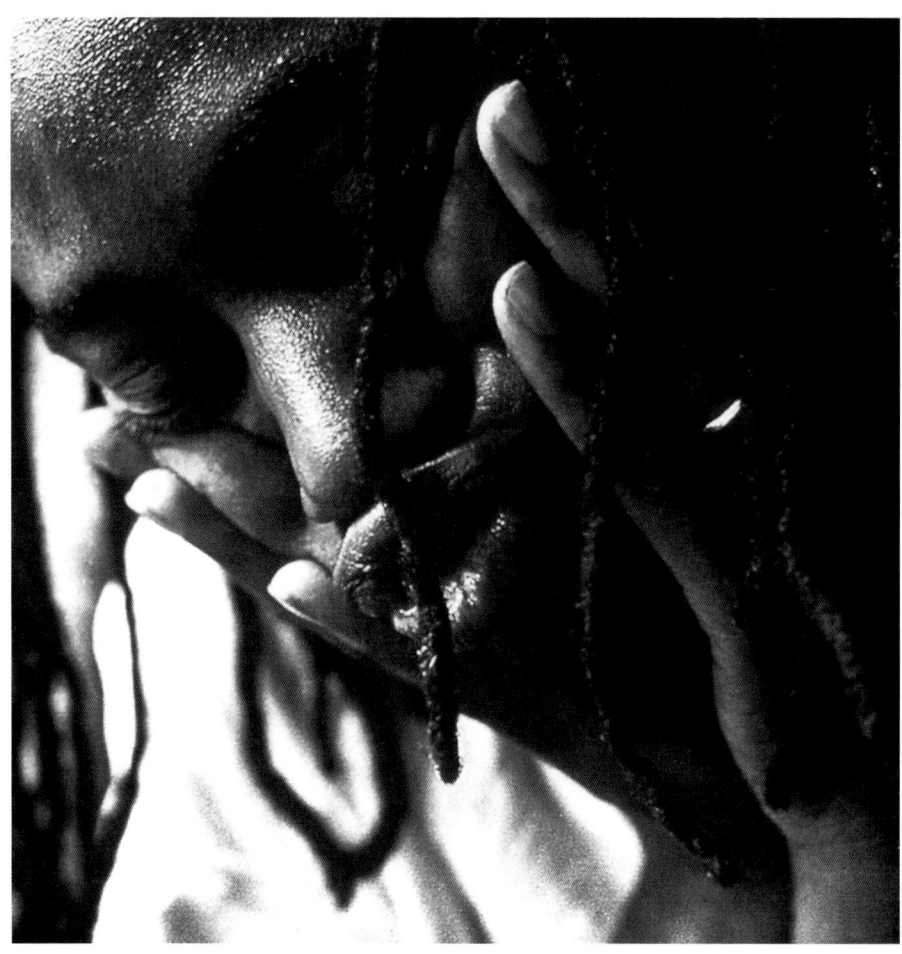

They're Almost Like Twins 1995
Inkjet prints on vinyl
Dimensions variable

OVERLEAF & P.70
Black Female Hairstyles 1995
50 collages on paper; 25 of
which are landscape (overleaf), 25 portrait (p.70)
Each 113 × 156.5/156.5 × 113

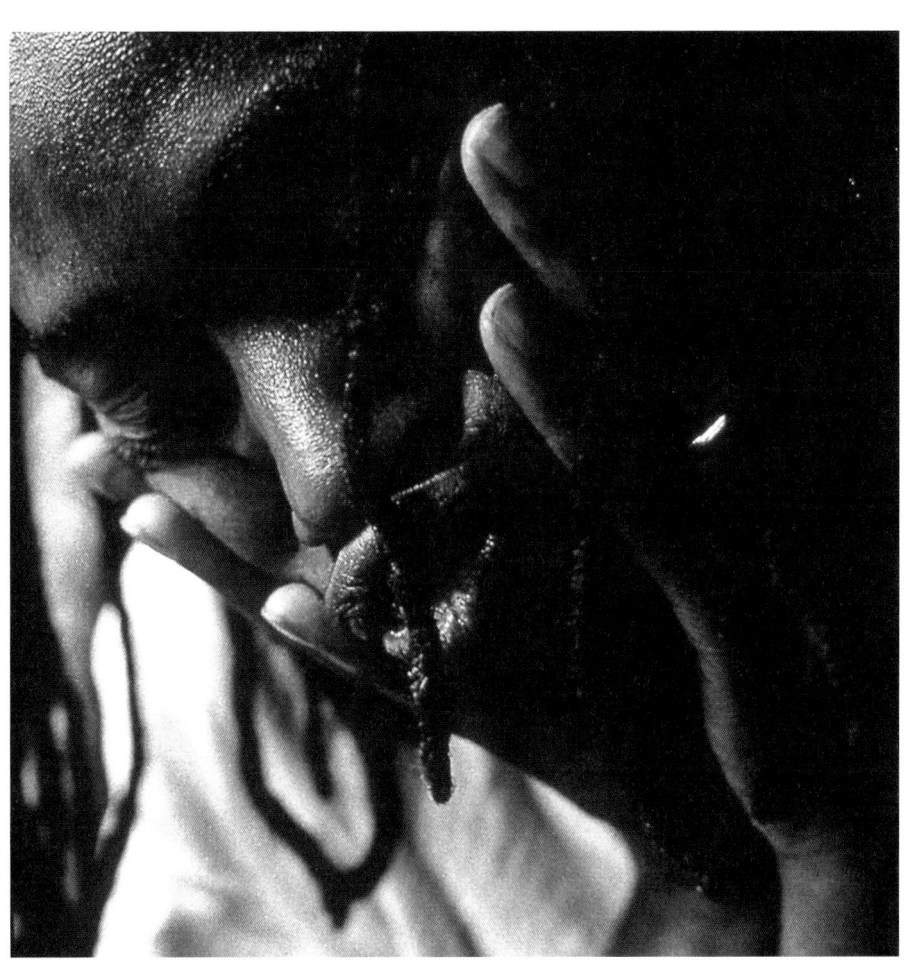

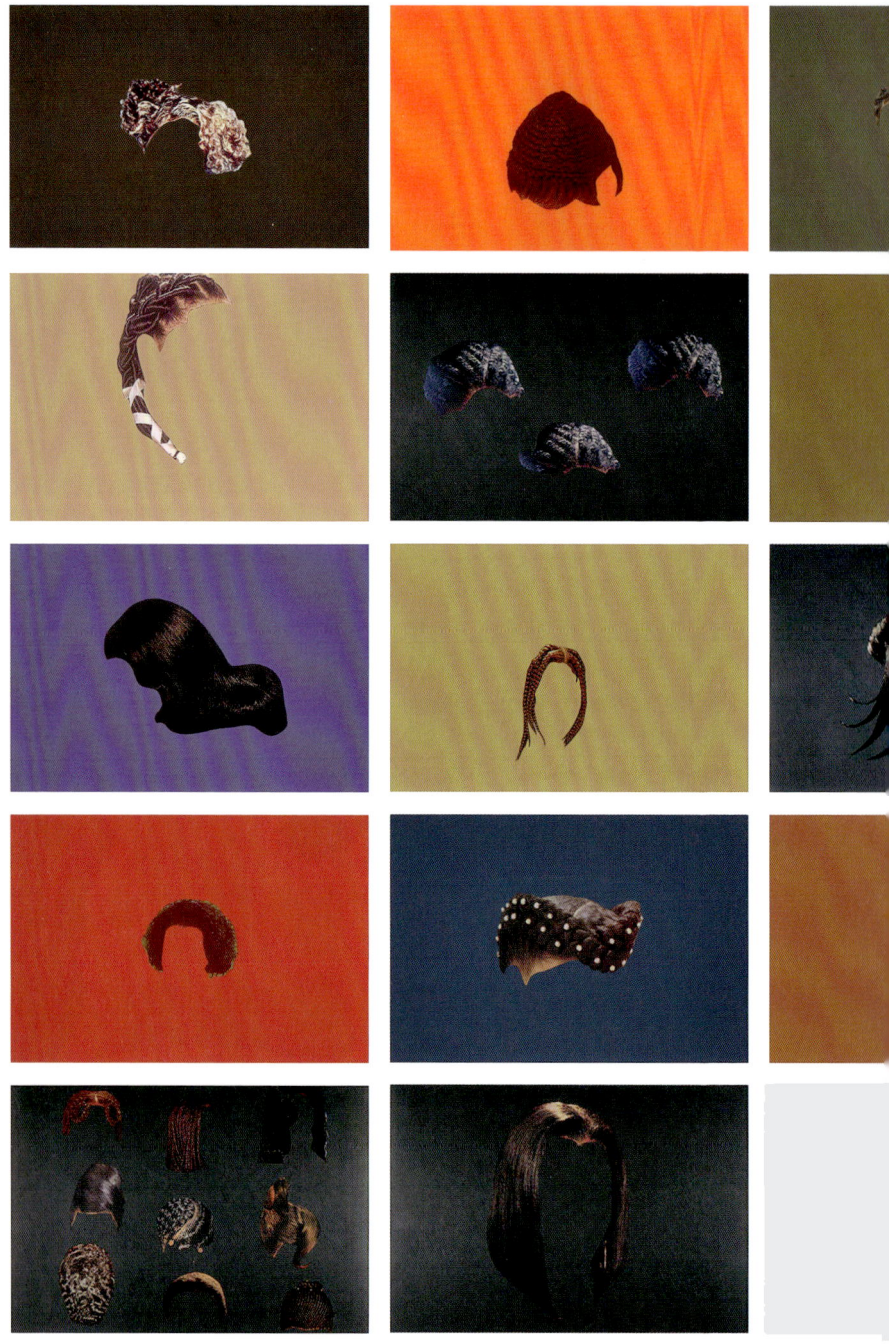

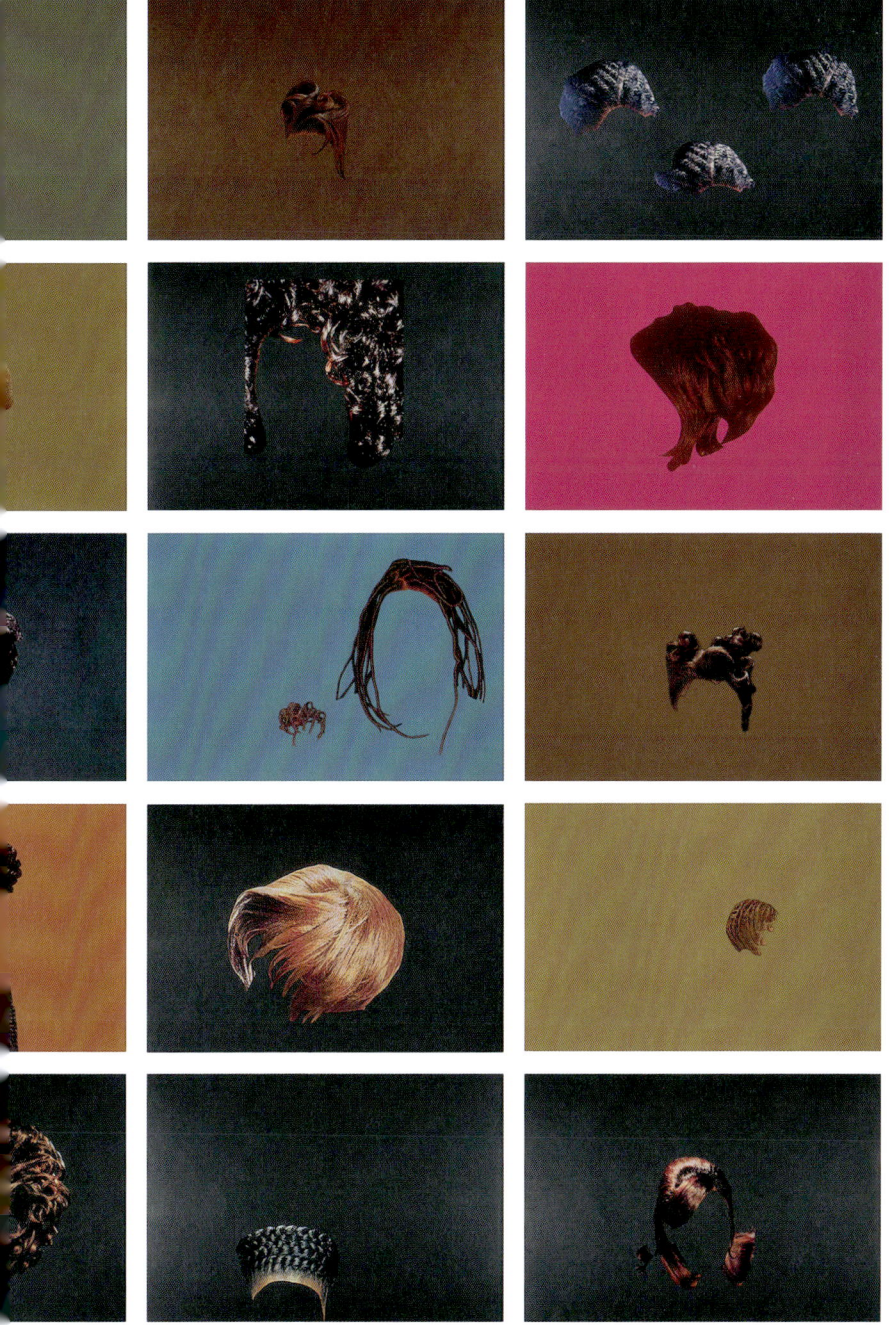

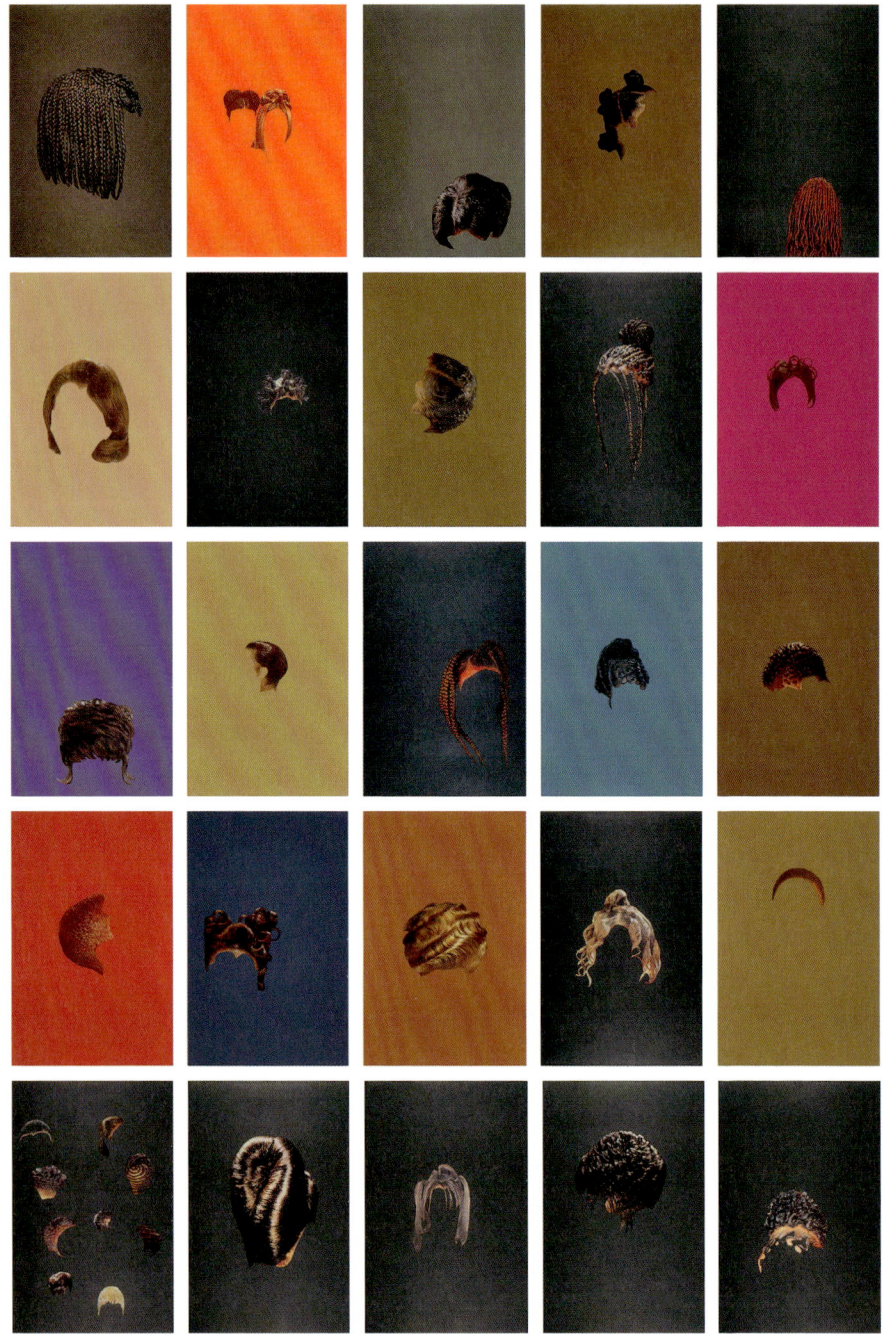

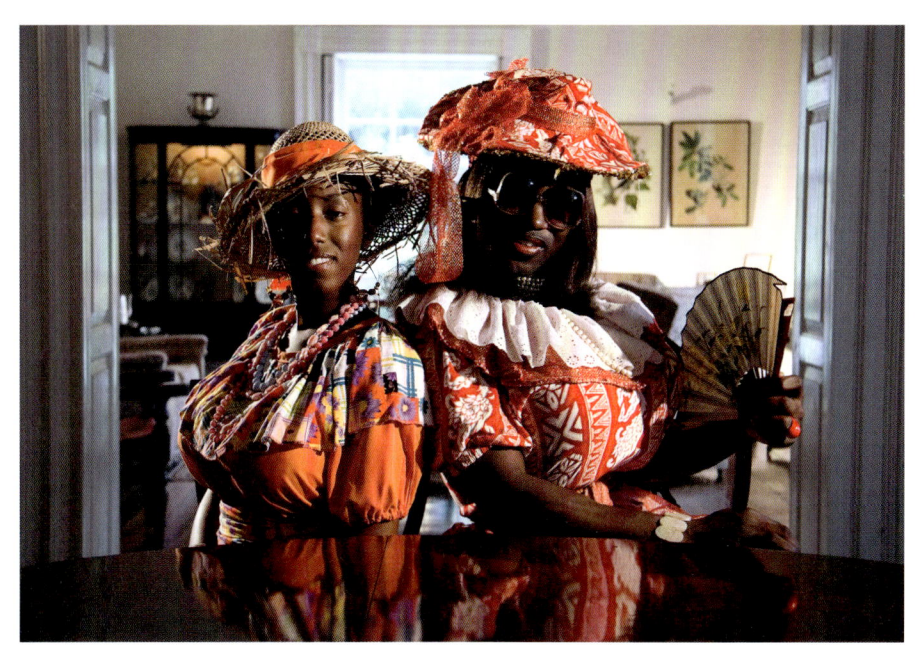

Crop Over 2007
Two-channel HD colour
video with sound
15 mins

OVERLEAF
For you, only you 2007
Three-channel colour
video with sound
15 mins
Installation view, Iniva,
Rivington Place, London,
2013

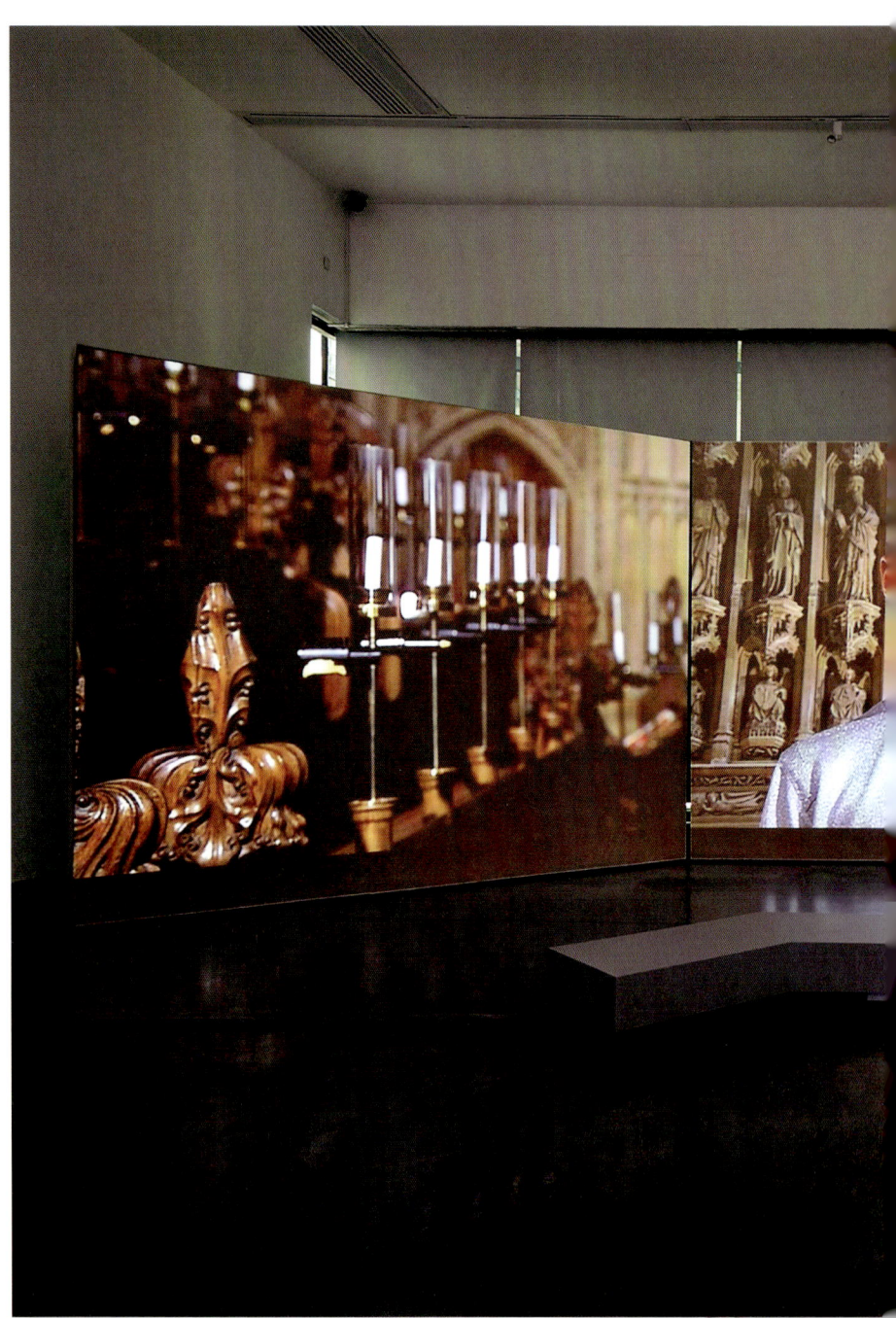

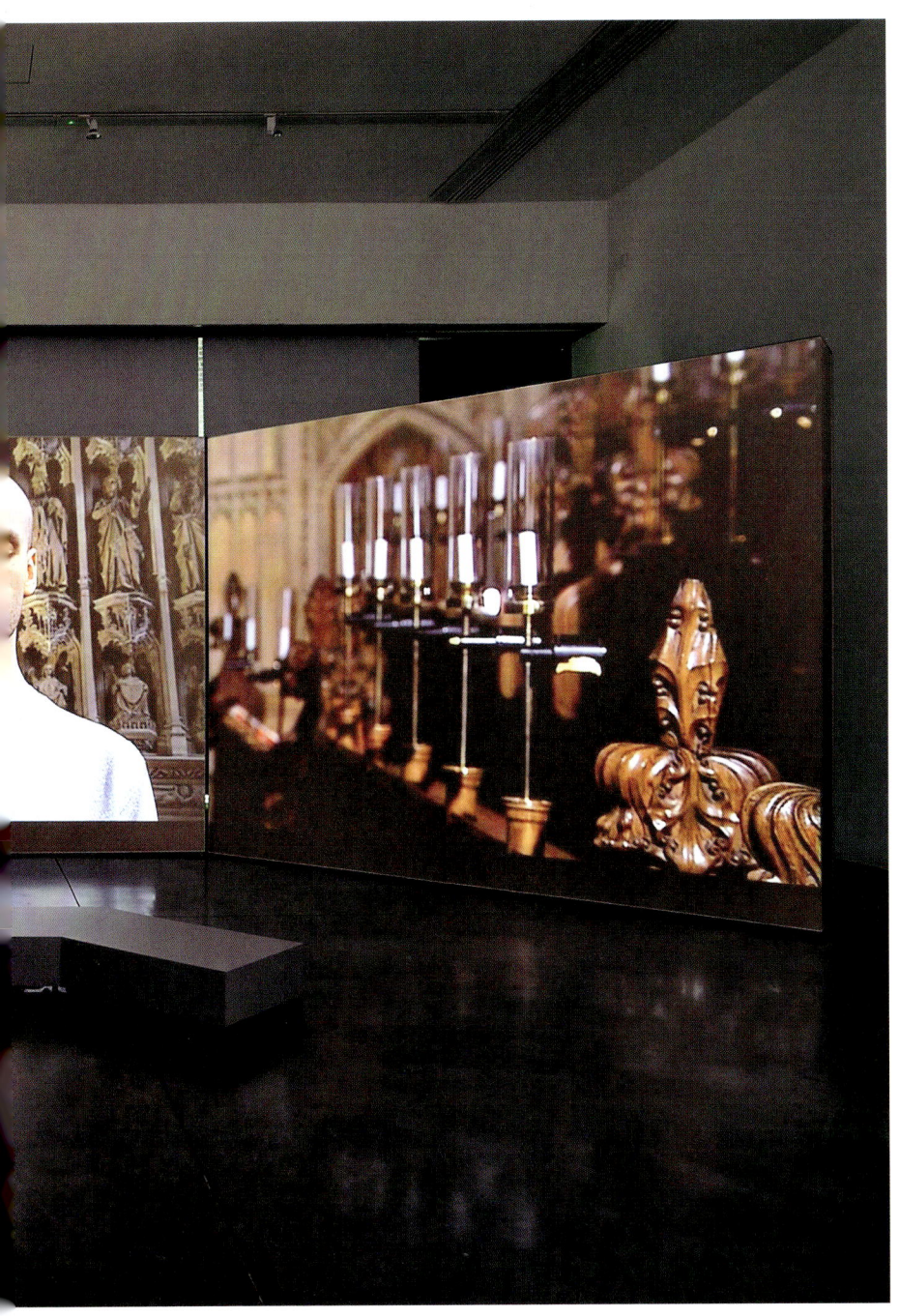

with Ain Bailey
Oh Adelaide 2010
Single-channel HD video
with sound
7 mins, 28 secs

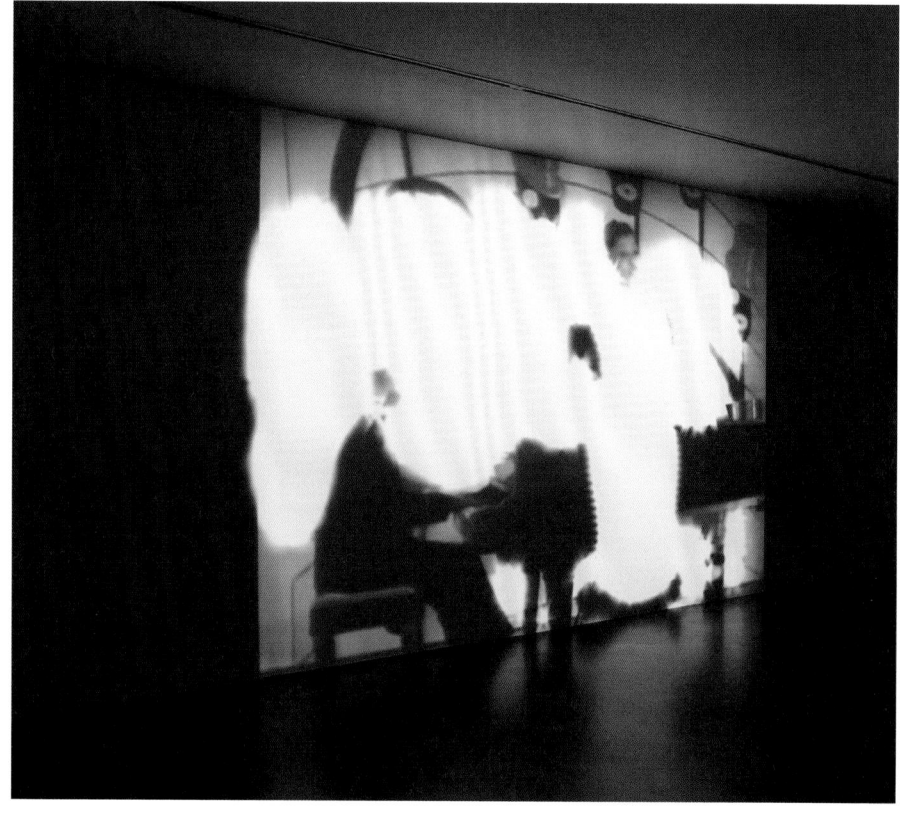

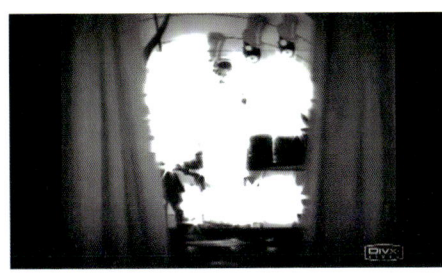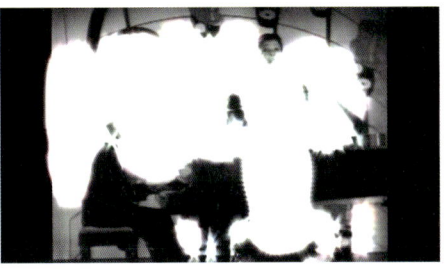

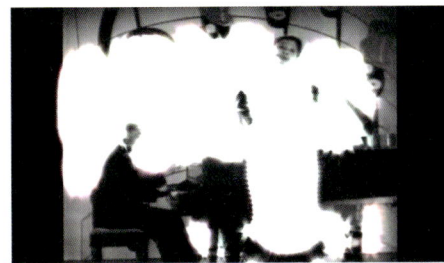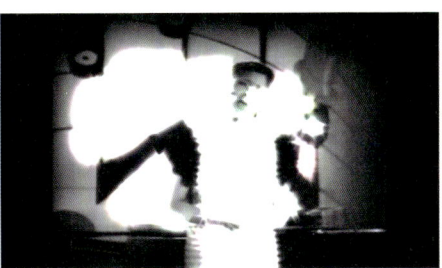

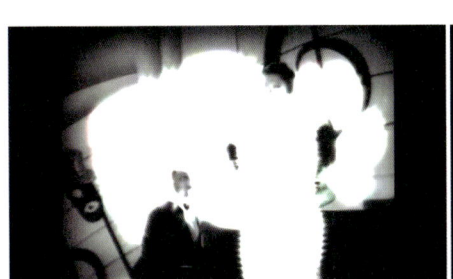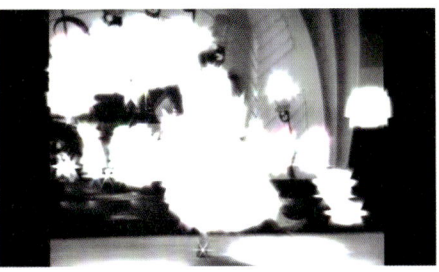

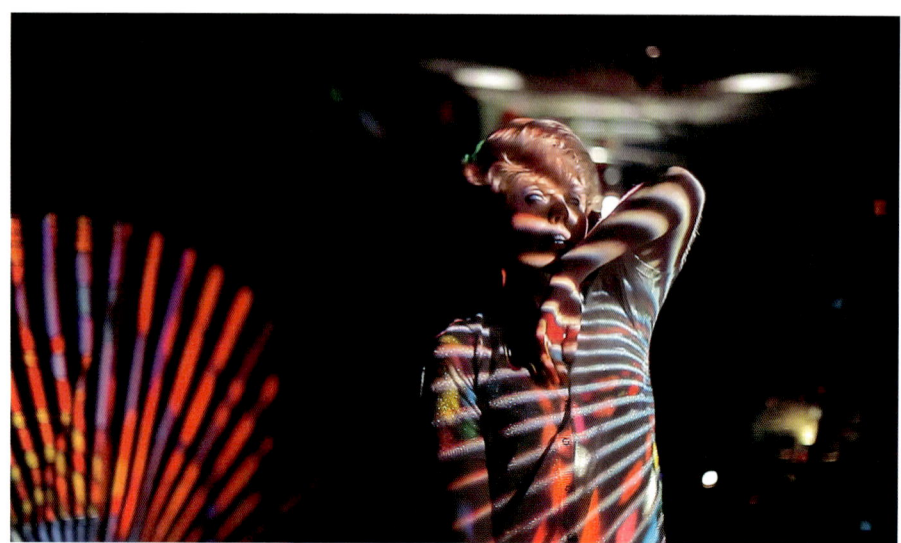

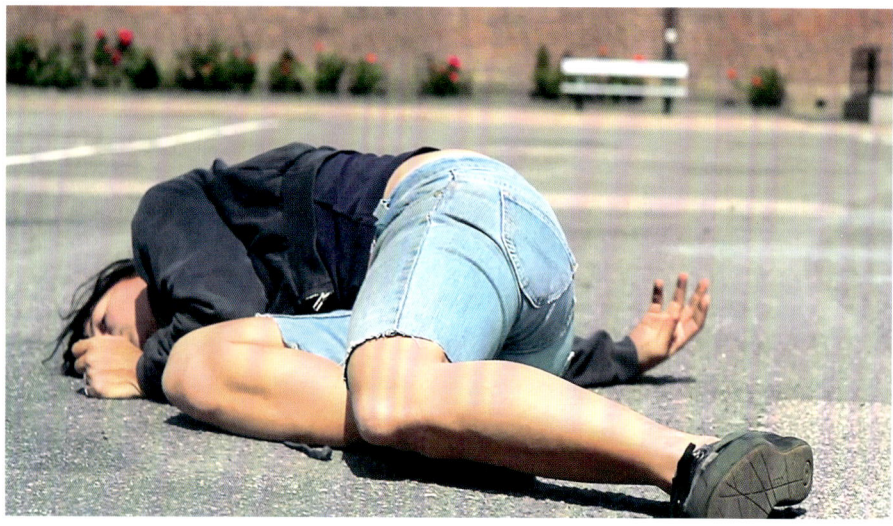

Move 2013
Single-channel HD colour
video with sound
11 mins

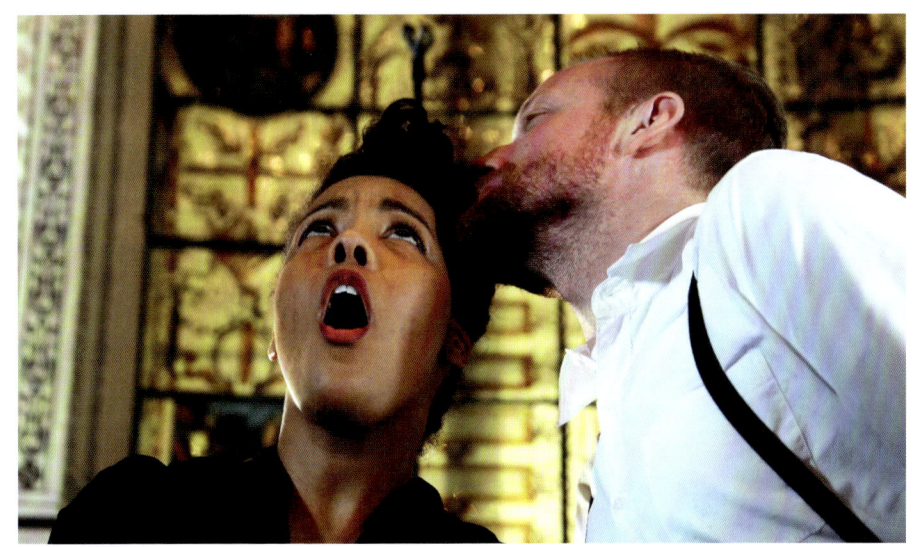

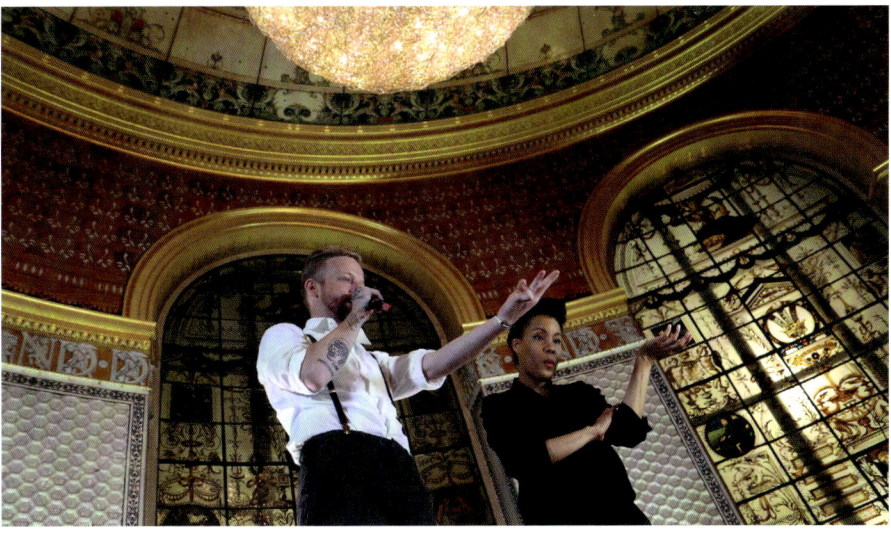

Exquisite Cacophony 2015
Single-channel HD colour
video with sound
35 mins

OVERLEAF
*Paper Tiger Whisky Soap
Theatre (Dada Nice)* 2016
Nine-channel HD colour
video installation with
sound and wallpaper
18 mins
Installation view, Villa
Arson, Nice, France 2016

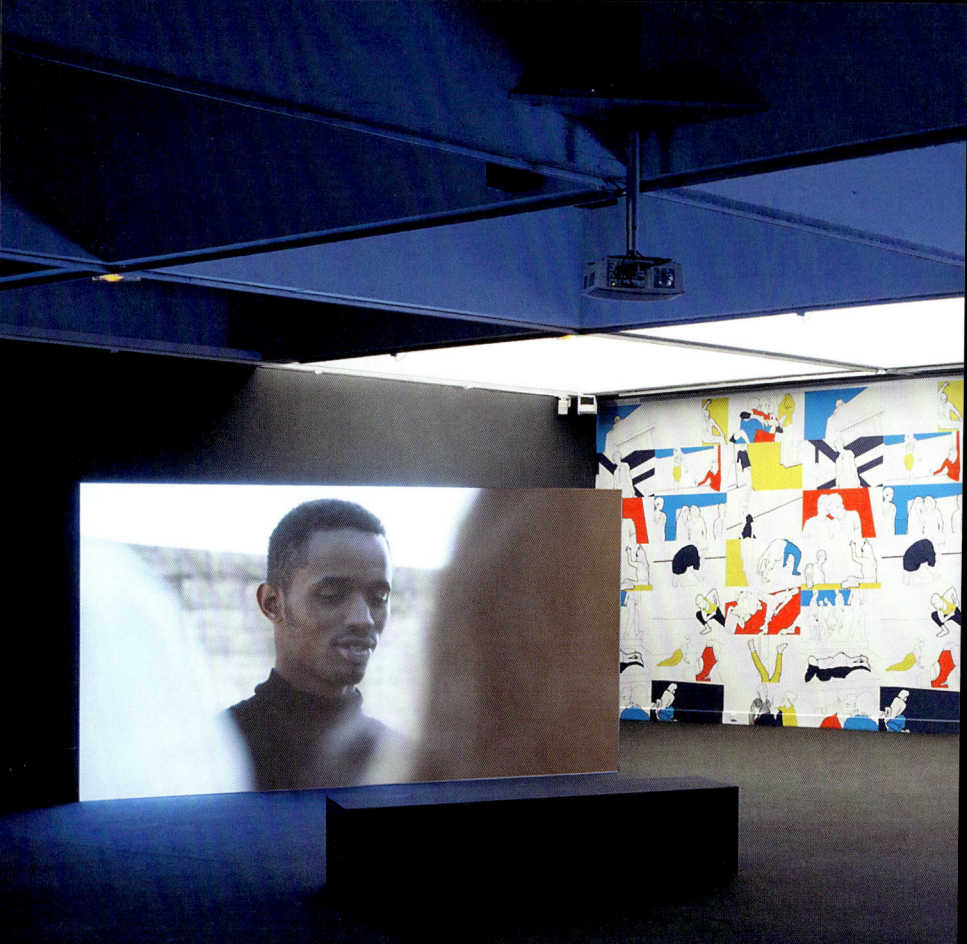

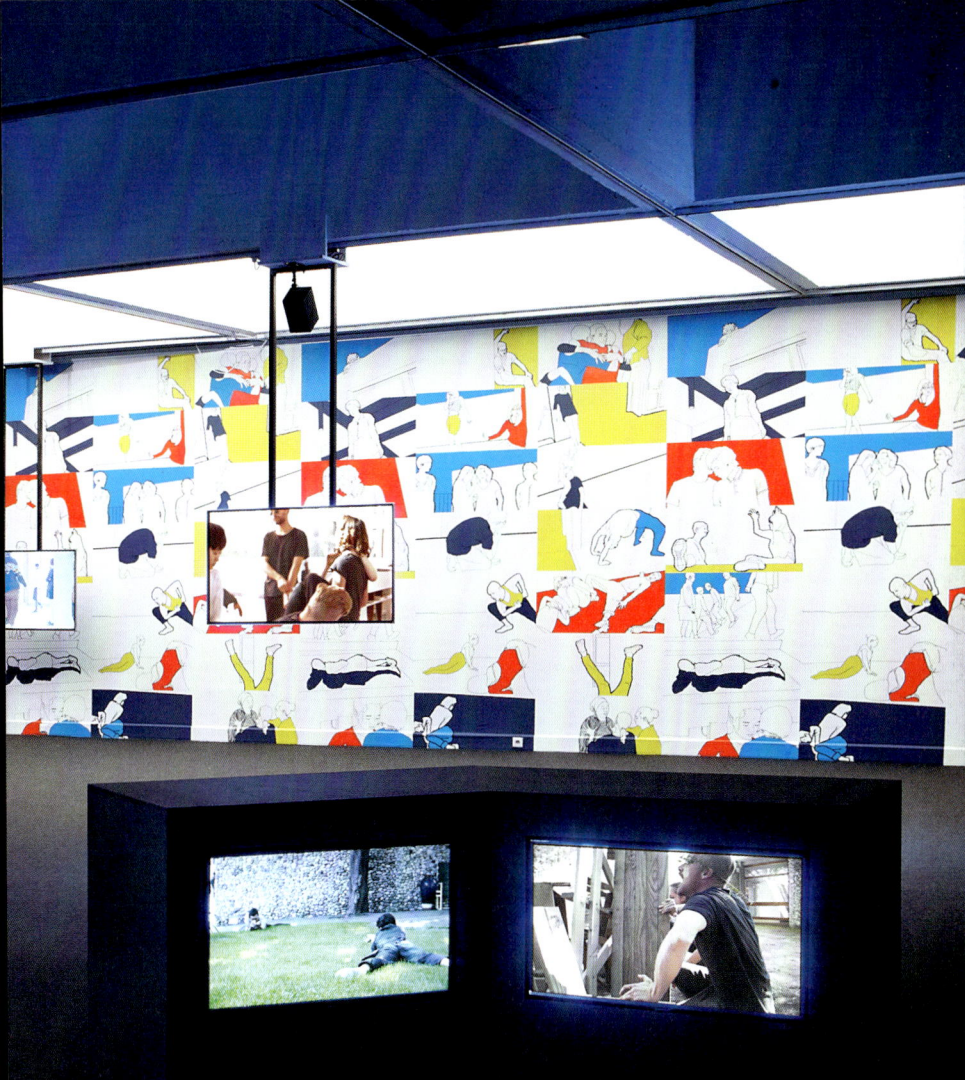

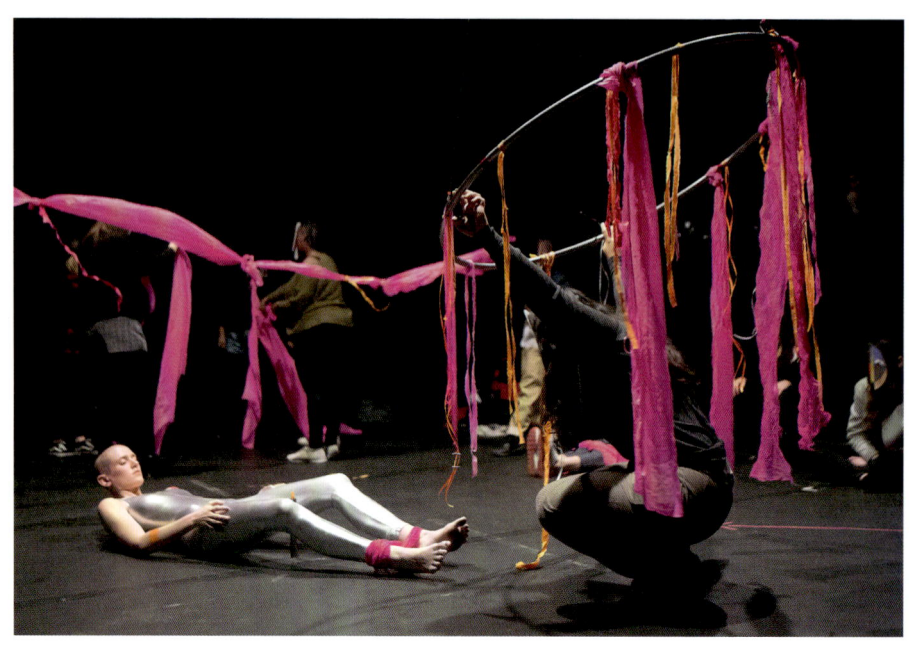

We move in her way 2017
Photographs documenting
the performance, Institute
of Contemporary Arts
(ICA), London, 2016

OVERLEAF
We move in her way 2017
Seven synchronised videos
with sound
18 mins
Installation view, ICA,
London, 2017

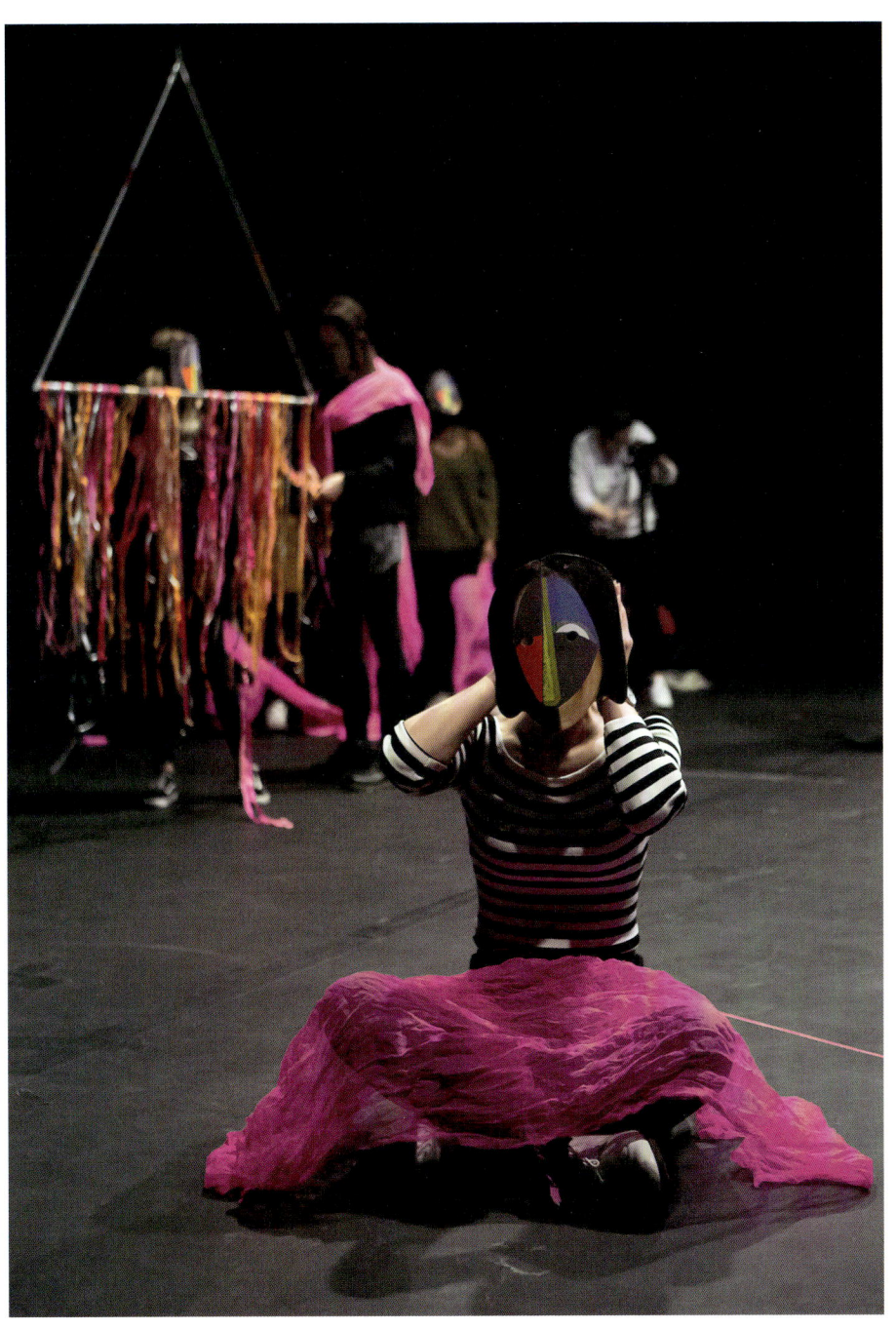

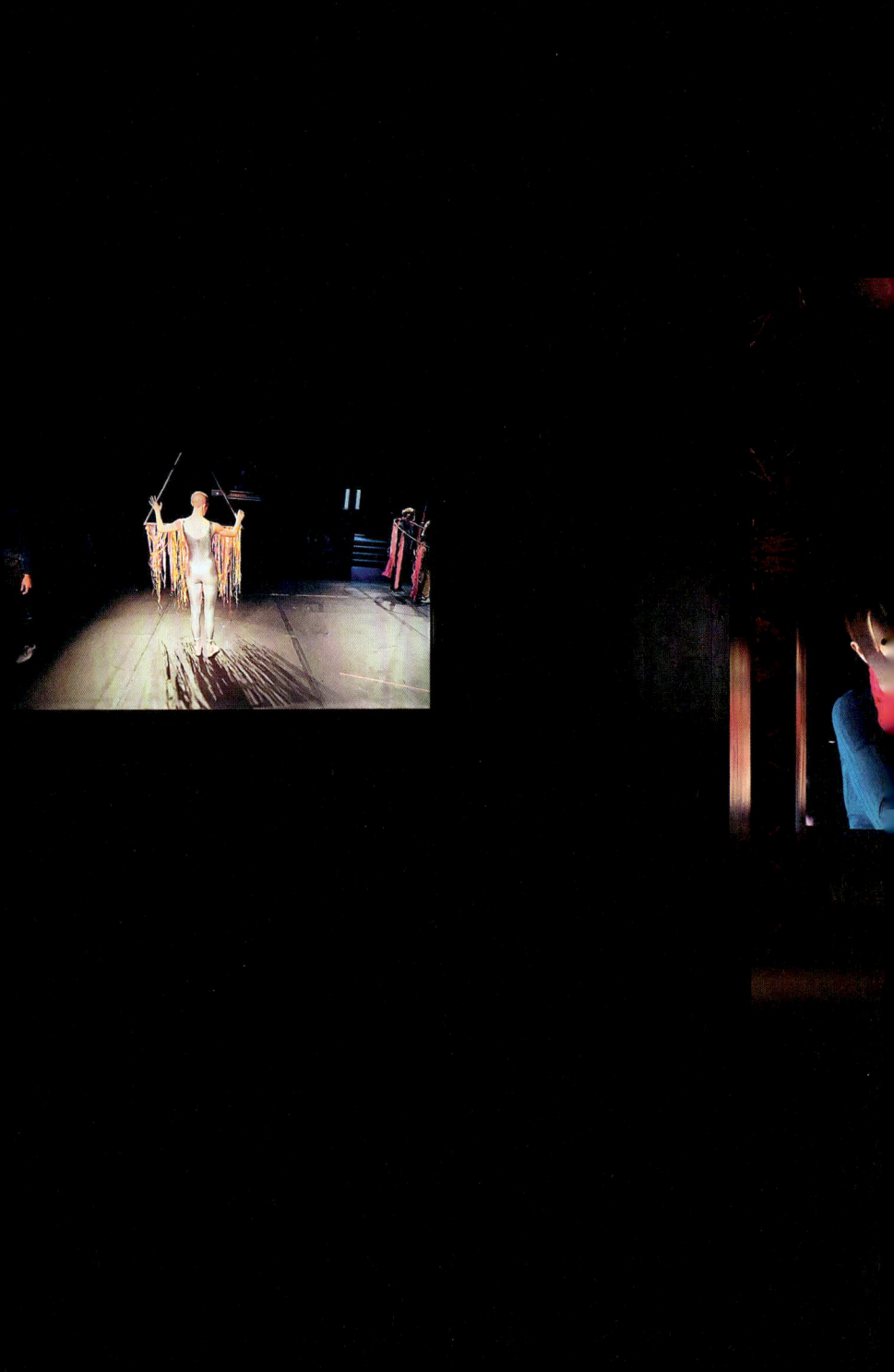

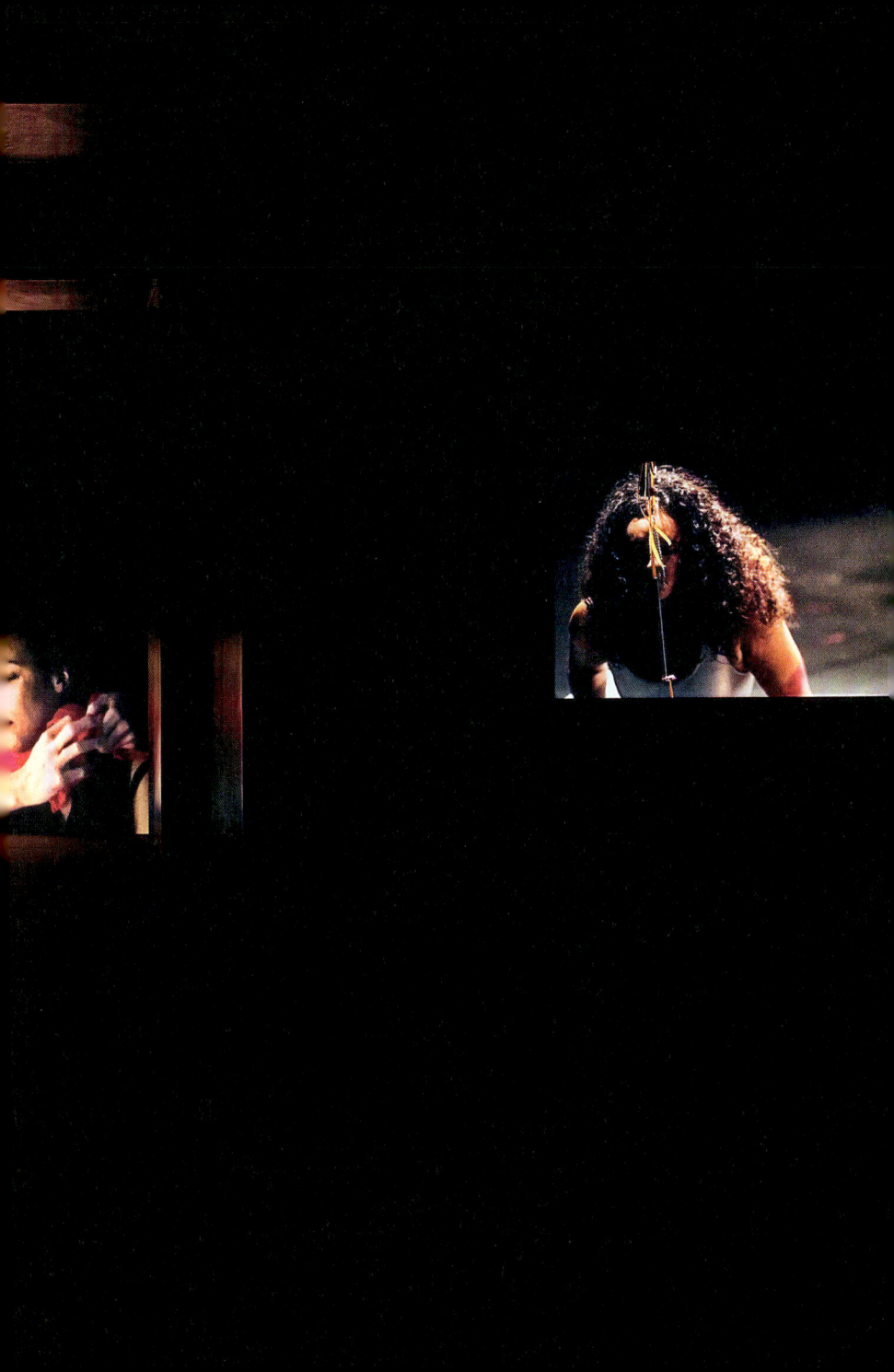

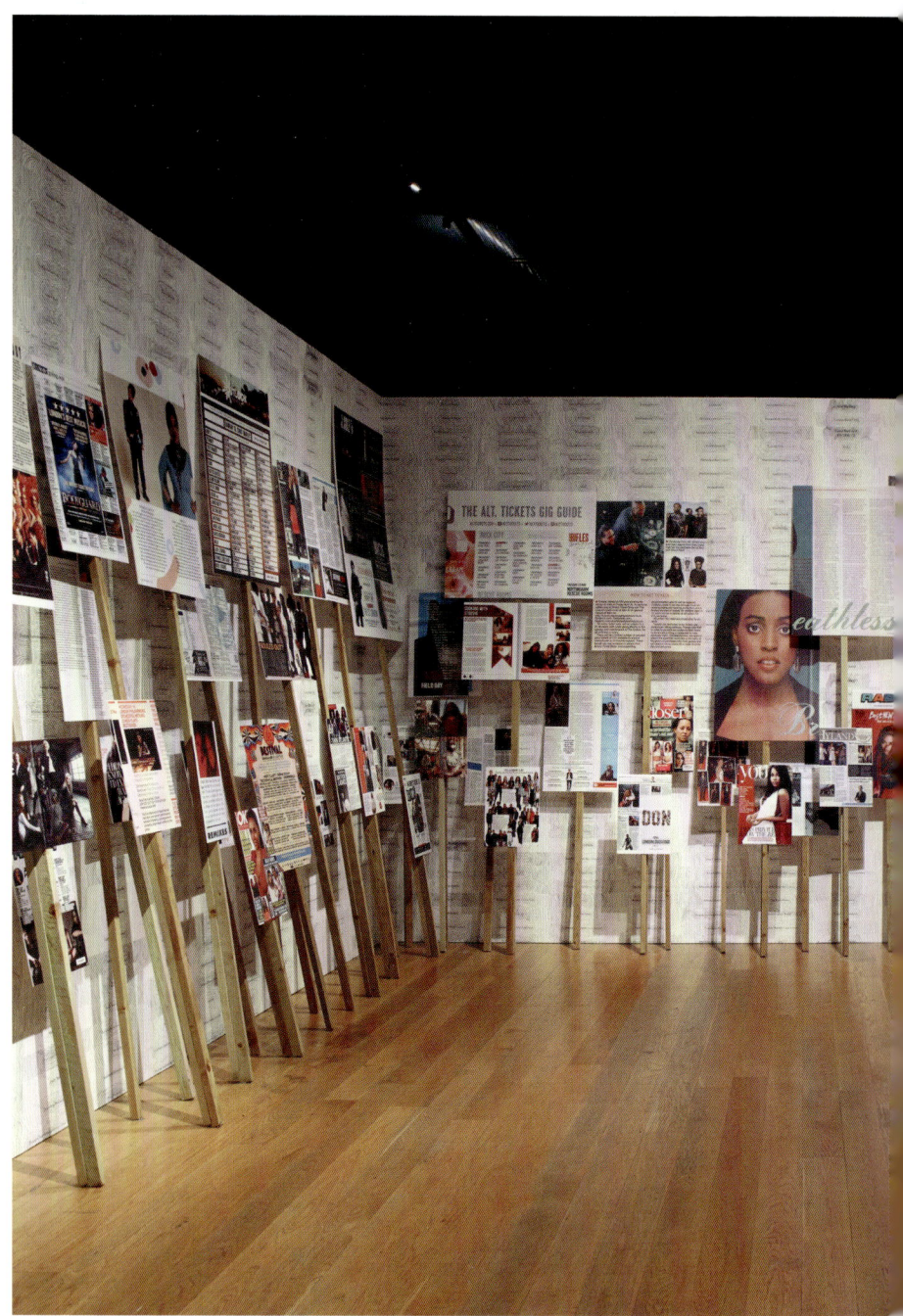

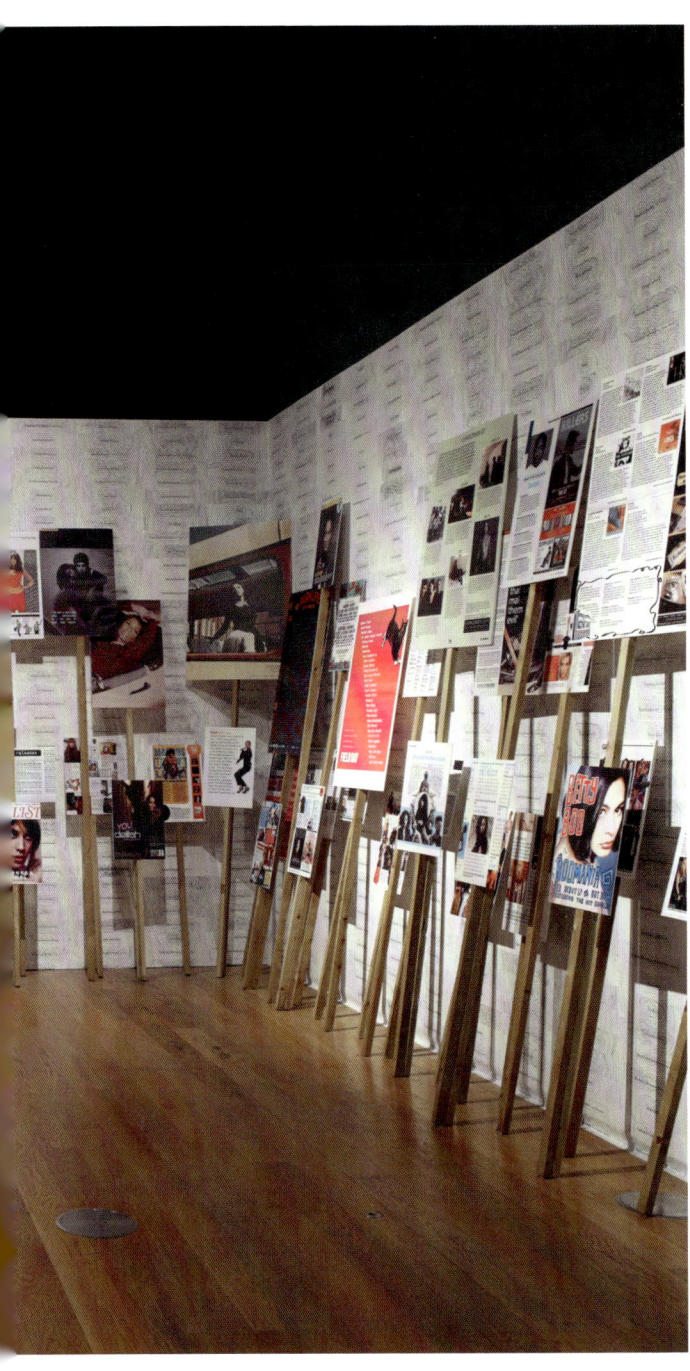

Devotional Wallpaper and Placards 2018
Digital prints on Correx and wood
Dimensions variable
Installation view,
Manchester Art Gallery,
Manchester, UK, 2018

OVERLEAF
Devotional Wallpaper (detail)
2017
Digital print on paper
One repeat: 500 × 200

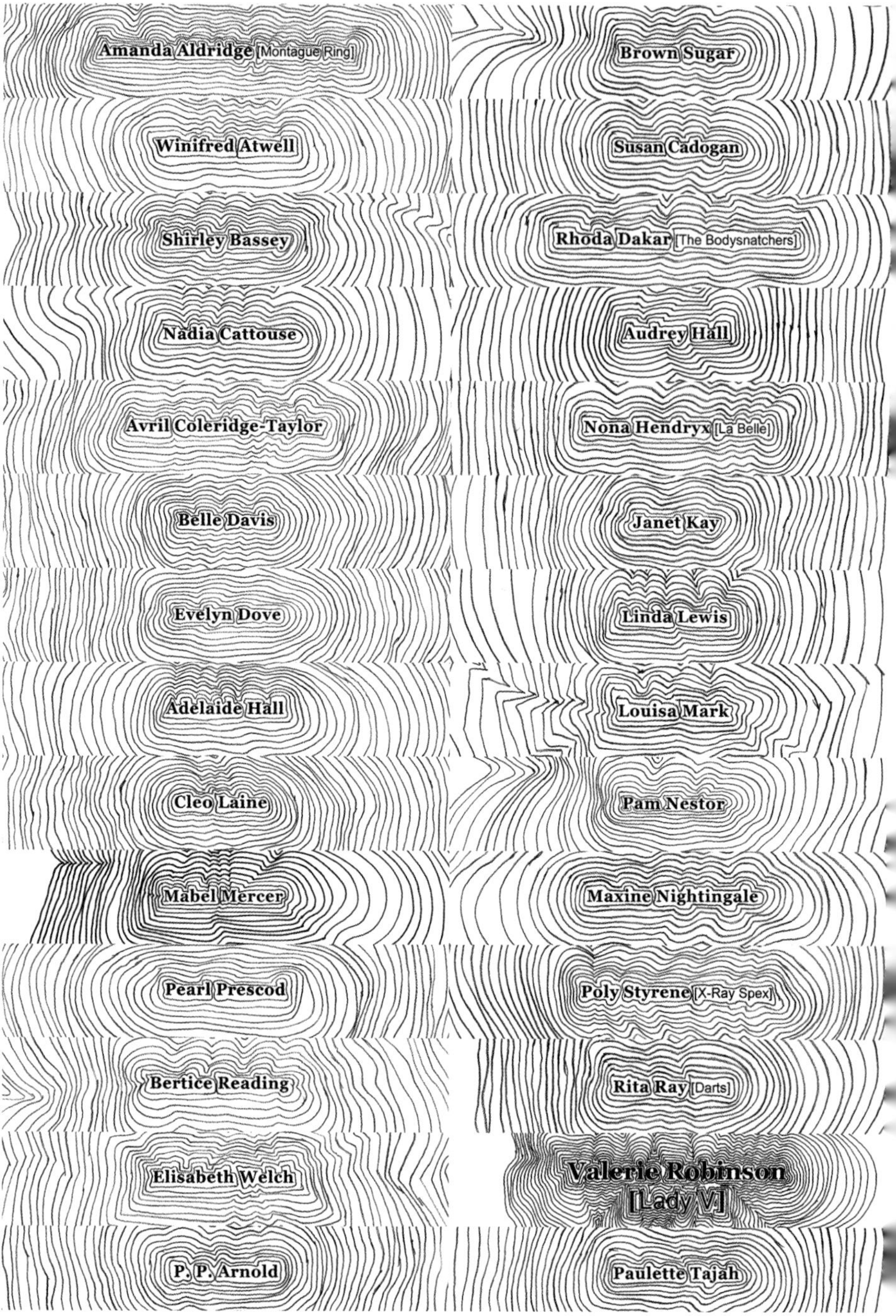

Amanda Aldridge [Montague Ring]

Brown Sugar

Winifred Atwell

Susan Cadogan

Shirley Bassey

Rhoda Dakar [The Bodysnatchers]

Nadia Cattouse

Audrey Hall

Avril Coleridge-Taylor

Nona Hendryx [La Belle]

Belle Davis

Janet Kay

Evelyn Dove

Linda Lewis

Adelaide Hall

Louisa Mark

Cleo Laine

Pam Nestor

Mabel Mercer

Maxine Nightingale

Pearl Prescod

Poly Styrene [X-Ray Spex]

Bertice Reading

Rita Ray [Darts]

Elisabeth Welch

Valerie Robinson [Lady V.]

P. P. Arnold

Paulette Tajah

86

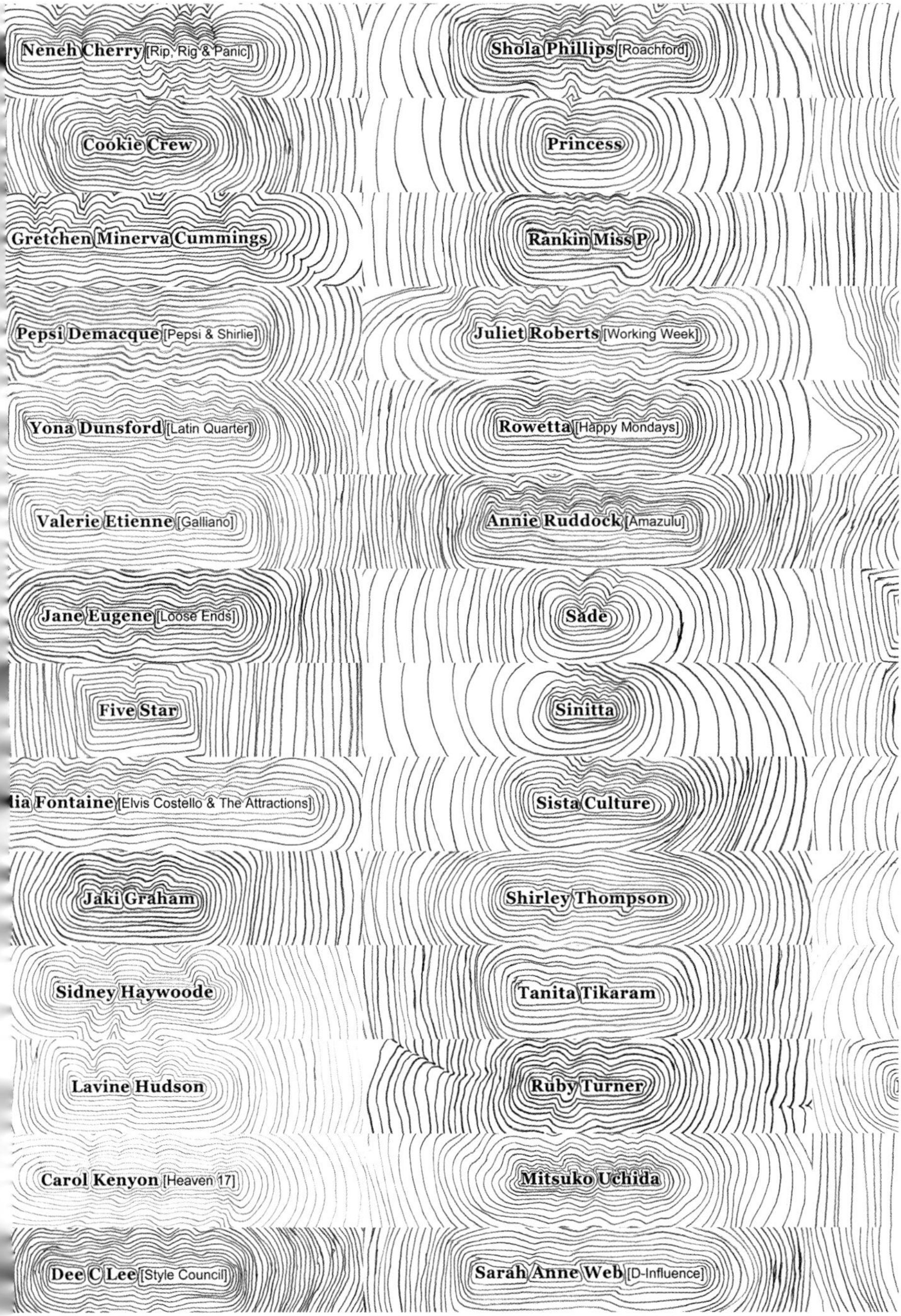

Neneh Cherry [Rip, Rig & Panic]

Shola Phillips [Roachford]

Cookie Crew

Princess

Gretchen Minerva Cummings

Rankin Miss P

Pepsi Demacque [Pepsi & Shirlie]

Juliet Roberts [Working Week]

Yona Dunsford [Latin Quarter]

Rowetta [Happy Mondays]

Valerie Etienne [Galliano]

Annie Ruddock [Amazulu]

Jane Eugene [Loose Ends]

Sade

Five Star

Sinitta

...ia Fontaine [Elvis Costello & The Attractions]

Sista Culture

Jaki Graham

Shirley Thompson

Sidney Haywoode

Tanita Tikaram

Lavine Hudson

Ruby Turner

Carol Kenyon [Heaven 17]

Mitsuko Uchida

Dee C Lee [Style Council]

Sarah Anne Web [D-Influence]

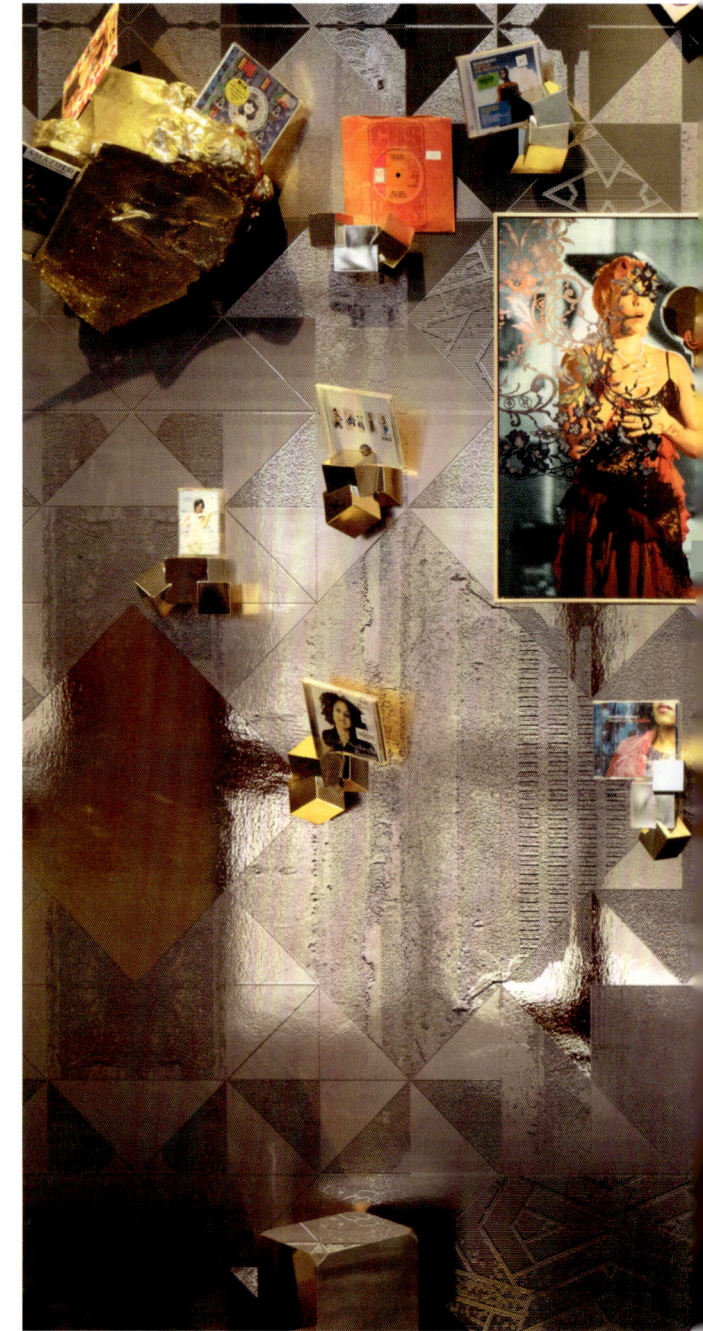

FEELING HER WAY 2022
Ten-channel ultra-HD video
installation with sound,
wallpapers and sculpture
Dimensions variable
Installation view at the 59th
International Art Exhibition –
La Biennale di Venezia,
Venice 2022

OVERLEAF
We move in her way Eve and
Be Wallpaper 2017
Digital print on vinyl
Dimensions variable

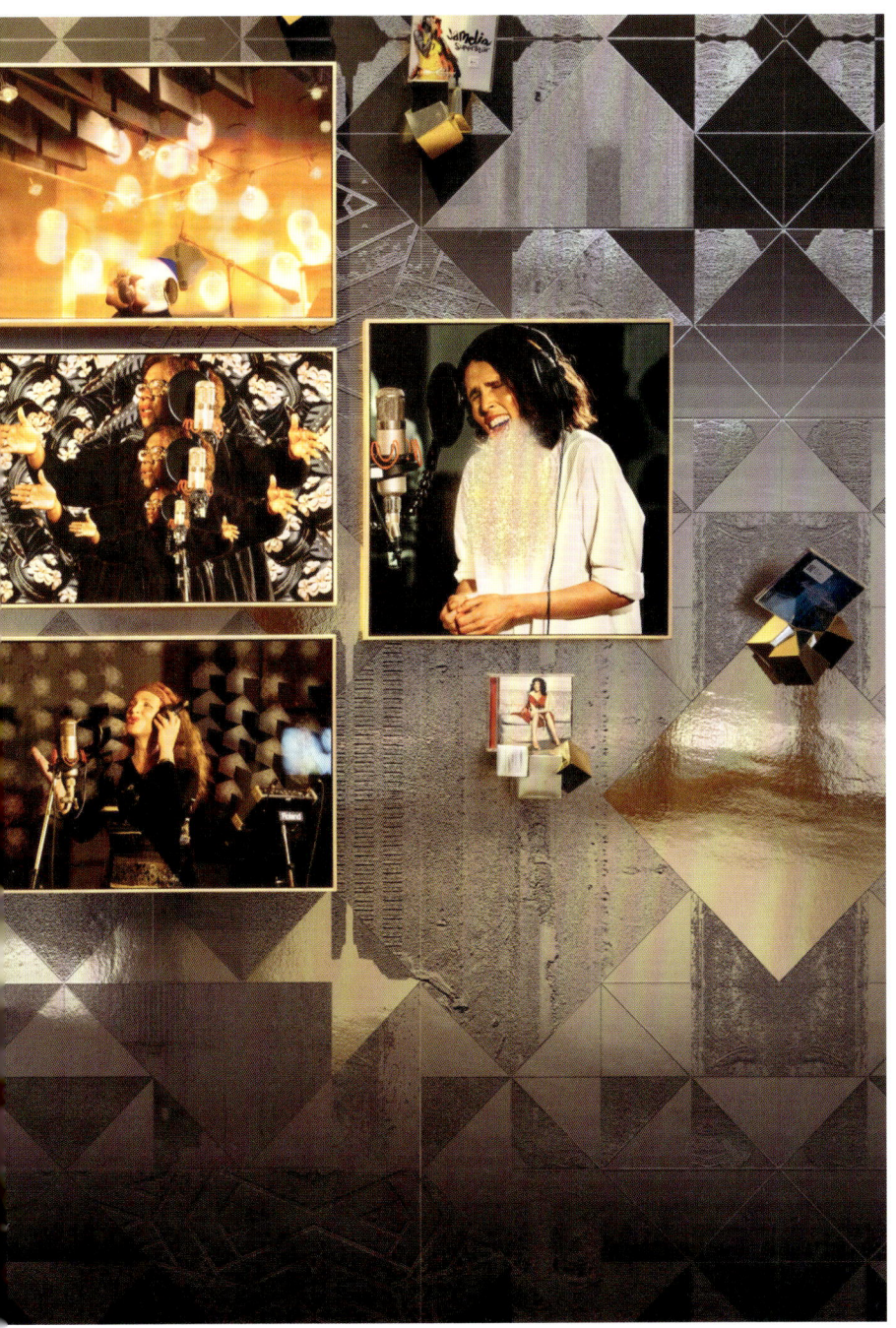

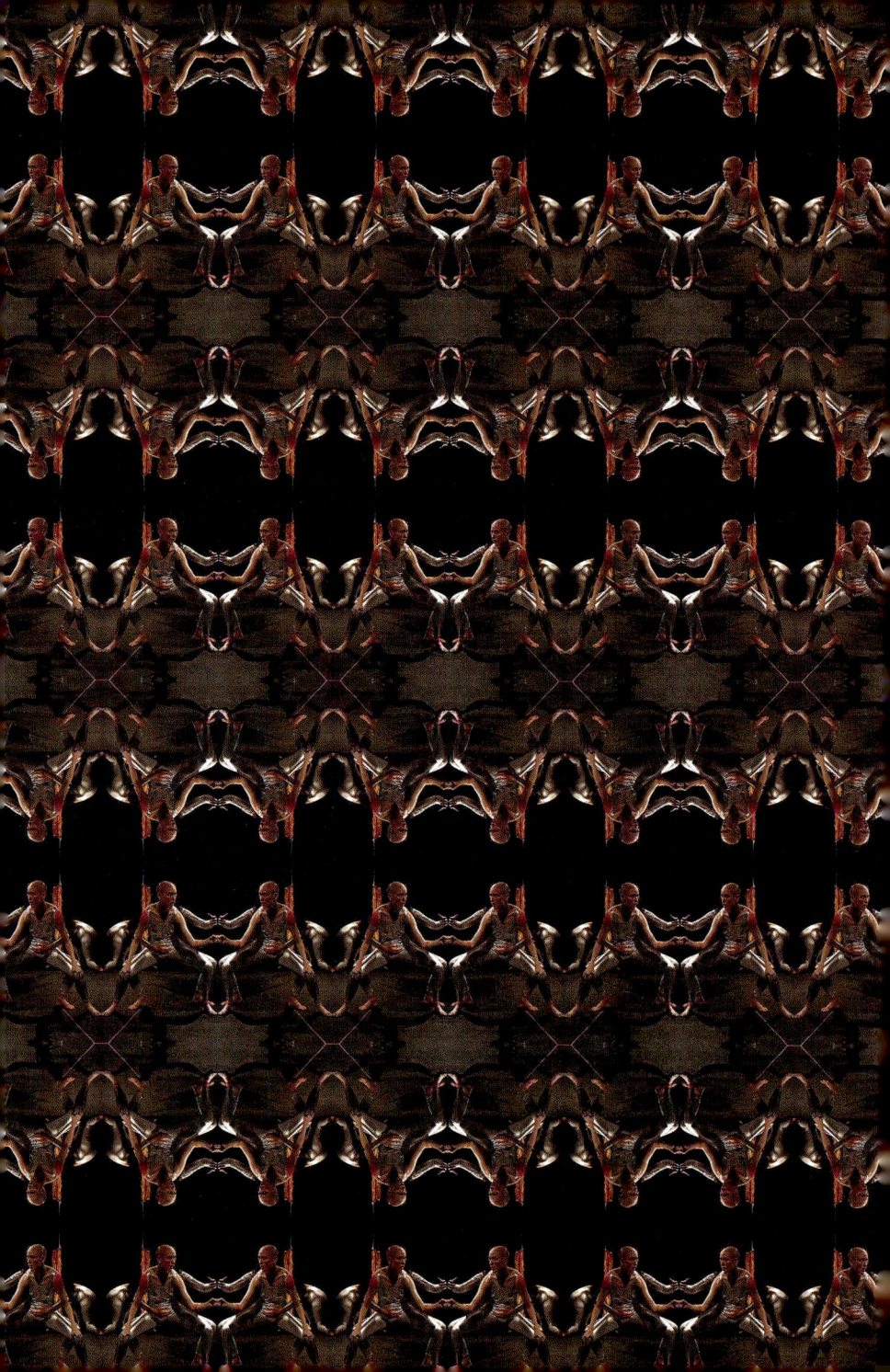

NOTES

1. See Christine Checinska, 'Spinning a Yarn of One's Own', in Jennifer Harris (ed.), *A Companion to Textile Culture*, Hoboken, NJ 2020, pp.241–2.

2. Courtney J. Martin, 'Interview: Sonia Boyce', in Emma Ridgway and Courtney J. Martin, *Sonia Boyce: Feeling Her Way*, London and New Haven, CT 2022, p.15.

3. Stourbridge College of Technology and Art would merge with Birmingham Metropolitan College in 2013.

4. Among Boyce's tutors was David Bainbridge, one of the founding members of Art & Language.

5. Martin 2022, p.19.

6. Boyce saw Hiller's show at Ikon Gallery, Birmingham in 1981; Hiller's project *Sisters of Menon* 1972–9 utilised automatic writing and mediumistic telepresence as part of a collective drawing project with other women.

7. Sonia Boyce, 'Extracts from a conversation with Pitika Ntuli', in *Sonia Boyce*, exh. cat., AIR Gallery, London 1986. Reproduced in Alice Correia (ed.), *What is Black Art?*, London 2022, p.127.

8. Sharon Smith, 'Black feminism and intersectionality', *International Socialist Review*, no.91, Winter 2023–4, https://isreview. org/issue/91/black-feminism-and-intersectionality/index.html, accessed 13 April 2024.

9. For a timeline of the development of the group, see David A. Bailey, Ian Baucom and Sonia Boyce (eds),

Shades of Black: Assembling Black Arts in 1980s Britain, London and Durham, NC 2002, from p.228.

10. Emma Ridgway, 'She Feels Her Way', in Ridgway and Martin 2022, p.50.

11. See Lubaina Himid, 'Preface' and 'Afterward', *The Thin Black Line: An exhibition curated by Lubaina Himid*, exh. cat., ICA, London 1985, p.12 and back cover.

12. See Martin 2022, p.16.

13. Sonia Boyce, statement published in *The Thin Black Line*, exh. cat., ICA, London 1985, p.9.

14. Kahlo's work was exhibited at the Whitechapel Gallery alongside Tina Modotti's photography in an exhibition curated by Laura Mulvey and Peter Wollen, running 26 March – 2 May 1982.

15. Sonia Boyce, 'Extracts from a conversation with Pitika Ntuli', in Correia (ed.) 2022, p.127.

16. See Anjalie Dalal-Clayton, 'Sonia Boyce: Beyond Blackness', NKA *Journal of Contemporary African Art*, no.45, Nov. 2019, pp.62–73.

17. John Roberts, 'Sonia Boyce: In Conversation with John Roberts', *Third Text*, no.1, 2008, pp.55–64 (p.64).

18. Conversation with author, 27 July 2023.

19. Martin 2022, p.19.

20. Ibid.; and Correia (ed.) 2022, p.126.

21. Kobena Mercer, 'Romare Bearden, 1964: Collage as Kunstwollen', in

Kobena Mercer (ed.), *Cosmopolitan Modernisms*, London and Cambridge, MA 2005, p.126; and Kobena Mercer, 'The Longest Journey: Black Diaspora Artists in Britain', *Art History*, vol.44, no.2, June 2021, pp.482–505 (p.503).

22. Sonia Boyce, 'Late Night Shopping, 3 October 1990', *The Invisible City*, exh. cat., The Photographer's Gallery, London 1990, n.p.

23. Ian Baucom, 'Every bit of it. All complete', in *The Unmapped Body: 3 Black British Artists*, exh. cat., Yale University Art Gallery, New Haven, CT 1998, p.9. While in his text Baucom refers to Stuart Hall's use of the expression 'the burden of representation', Mercer first adopted it and cemented its use in his influential essay 'Black art and the burden of representation', *Third Text*, vol.4. no.10, 61–78, https://doi. org/10.1080/0952882900 8576253, accessed 14 April 2024.

24. The collected papers of the Iniva founding symposium 'A New Internationalism', held at the Tate Gallery, London in April 1994, were published as Jean Fisher (ed.), *Global Visions: Towards a New Internationalism in the Visual Arts*, London 1994.

25. David Chandler, 'Introduction', *The Invisible City*, exh. cat., The Photographer's Gallery, London 1990, n.p.

26. Gilane Tawadros, *Speaking in Tongues*, London 1997, p.7.

27. See Nizan Shaked, 'Sonia Boyce: Reclassifying Classification', *Afterall*, no.49, Spring/Summer 2020, https://

www.afterall.org/articles/
sonia-boyce-reclassify-
ing-classification, accessed
14 April 2024.

28. Tawadros 1997, p.20.

29. See Alice Mahon,
*Surrealism and the Politics
of Eros, 1938–1968*, London
2005, pp.152–63.

30. Baucom 1998, p.12.

31. Sonia Boyce, excerpt
from the artist's application
statement for a residency
at Manchester University,
reproduced in Mark
Crinson (ed.), *Sonia Boyce:
Performance*, London 1998,
p.44.

32. Quoted in Elena Crippa,
'In Depth: *The Audition*
1997, printed 2018', Tate,
October 2018, https://www.
tate.org.uk/art/artworks/
boyce-the-audition-p82514,
accessed 15 April 2024.

33. Michel Serres, *Statues:
Le seconde livre des fondations*,
Paris 1989, pp.207, 227;
and Michel Serres, *The
Parasite*, trans. by Lawrence
R. Schehr, London and
Minneapolis, MN 2007,
pp.229, 233.

34. Linda Nochlin, *The Body
in Pieces: The Fragment as a
Metaphor of Modernity*, New
York 1995, pp.7–23.

35. Ibid., p.53.

36. Sonia Boyce, in Rebecca
Fortnum (ed.), *Contemporary
British Women Artists in their
Own Words*, London 2010,
p.117.

37. Richard Hancock,
quoted in Sonia Boyce,
'Saastamoinen Foundation
Keynote 2022: Sonia
Boyce', transcript of lecture
delivered at Dance House
Helsinki, Helsinki, 14 Sept.
2022, the artist's private
archive, p.3.

38. See Claudia Rankine's
introduction to *On
Whiteness: The Racial
Imaginary Institute*, SPBH
Essays, no.4, 2022, pp.7–16.

39. Mark Crinson, 'Telling
Lyrics', in Crinson 1998,
p.27.

40. See Gustavus Stadler,
'"My Wife": The Tape
Recorder and Warhol's
Queer Ways of Listening',
Criticism, vol.56, no.3,
Summer 2014, pp.425–56;
and Jennifer Sichel, '"Do
you think Pop Art's queer?":
Gene Swenson and Andy
Warhol', *Oxford Art Journal*,
vol.41, no.1, March 2018,
pp.59–83.

41. See Cindy Moore,
'Why Feminists Can't Stop
Talking About Voice', *Com-
position Studies*, vol.30, no.2,
Autumn 2002, pp.11–25.

42. Claire Bishop,
'Introduction', in Claire
Bishop (ed.), *Participation*,
London 2006, p.12.

43. Boyce's *For you, only you*
was commissioned by the
Ruskin School of Drawing
& Fine Art, University of
Oxford, in partnership with
the De La Warr Pavilion,
Locus+, Milton Keynes
Gallery and Model Arts and
Niland Gallery, and with
the support of Arts Council
England.

44. As Boyce addressed in
her lecture 'Saastamoinen
Foundation Keynote 2022:
Sonia Boyce', dada's kinship
to jazz is discussed in Jed
Rasula, *Destruction Was My
Beatrice: Dada and the Unmak-
ing of the Twentieth Century*,
New York 2015.

45. A recording of John
Cage's interview and performance of 'Empty Words' on
8 Aug. 1974 is available at
https://archive.org/details/
Cage_interview_and_per-

formance_Empty_words_
August_1974_A002A,
accessed 15 April 2024.

46. Sonia Boyce, 'Some
sketches towards "Exquisite
Cacophony": Working
with Astronautalis and
Elaine Mitchener', video
documentation, the artist's
private archive.

47. Quoted in *Sonia Boyce
Reader*, Birmingham 2017,
https://eastsideprojects.
org/wp-content/uploads/
Sonia-Boyce-Reader1.pdf,
accessed 15 April 2024.

48. Jean Fisher, 'For You,
Only You: The Return of
the Troubadour', in Sophie
Orlando (ed.), *Sonia Boyce:
Thoughtful Disobedience*, Dijon
2017, p.46.

49. Boyce quoted in
'Encounters: Sonia Boyce
& Sophie Orlando', in ibid.,
p.129.

50. 'Letter from Lygia Clark
to Hélio Oiticica, 14
November 1968', published
in Bishop 2006, pp.114–15.

51. Sandra Paola López
Ramírez and Chris Reyman,
'Improvising New Realities:
Movement, Sound and
Social Therapeutics',
*Critical Studies in Improvisation
/ Études critiques en improv-
isation*, vol.12, no.1, 2018,
https://www.criticalimprov.
com/index.php/csieci/arti-
cle/view/3770, accessed
15 April 2024.

52. Ibid.

53. Adrian Piper, 'Notes
on Funk I' (1985), in
Adrian Piper (ed.), *Out of
Order, Out of Sight, Volume I:
Selected Writings in Meta-Art
1968–1992*, London and
Cambridge, MA 1996, p.195.

54. Poppy Ajudha quoted in
Ridgway 2022, p.125.

FURTHER READING

MONOGRAPHS & SOLO
EXHIBITION CATALOGUES

For You Only You, A Project by Sonia Boyce, exh. cat., Ruskin School of Drawing & Fine Art, University of Oxford, Oxford 2008. Texts by Paul Bonaventura and Jean Fisher; contributions by Sonia Boyce, Mikhail Karikis and David Skinner

Peep: Sonia Boyce, exh. cat., Royal Pavilion, Art Gallery and Museums, Brighton 1995. Texts by Anthony Shelton and Gilane Tawadros

Sonia Boyce, exh. cat., AIR Gallery, London 1986. Introduction by Pitika Ntuli and conversation with Sonia Boyce

Sonia Boyce: Like Love, exh. cat., Spike Island, Bristol, 2009 and Bluecoat, Liverpool, 2010, Berlin 2010. Texts by Zoë Shearman and Marie-Anne McQuay

Mark Crinson (ed.), *Sonia Boyce: Performance*, series title: *Annotations*, no.2, London 1998

Sophie Orlando (ed.), *Sonia Boyce: Thoughtful Disobedience*, Dijon 2017

Emma Ridgway and Courtney J. Martin, exh. cat., *Sonia Boyce: Feeling Her Way*, National Participation (Great Britain), 59th *International Art Exhibition, La Biennale di Venezia*, New Haven 2022

Gilane Tawadros, *Speaking in Tongues*, London 1997

SELECTED GROUP
EXHIBITION CATALOGUES

The Thin Black Line: An exhibition curated by Lubaina Himid, ICA, London 1985. Text by Lubaina Himid

The Invisible City, The Photographer's Gallery, London 1990. Text by David Chandler

Nick Aikens, Elizabeth Robles (eds), *The Place is Here: The Work of Black Artists in 1980s Britain*, exh. cat., Van Abbemuseum, Berlin and Eindhoven, 2019

Okwui Enwezor (ed.), *All the World's Future: 56th International Art Exhibition, La Biennale di Venezia*, Venice 2015

Christine Eyene (ed.), *Sounds Like Her, Gender, Sound Art & Sonic Cultures*, exh. cat., New Art Exchange, Nottingham, 2017–18; York Art Gallery, York, 2019; Gallery Oldham, Oldham, 2019–2020, Nottingham 2019. Texts by Christine Eyene, Cathy Lane, Salomé Voegelin

Alex Farquharson and David A. Bailey (eds), *Life Between Islands: Caribbean–British Art 1950s–Now*, exh. cat., Tate Britain, London 2021

Linsey Young, (ed.), *Women in Revolt!: Art and Activism in the UK 1970–90*, exh. cat., Tate Britain, London 2023

SELECTED JOURNALS
& ARTICLES

Sonia Boyce and Dorothy Price (eds), 'Rethinking British Art: Black Artists and Modernism', *Art History*, vol.44. no.3, 2021, pp.445–675

Anjalie Dalal-Clayton, 'Sonia Boyce: Beyond Blackness', NKA *Journal of Contemporary African Art*, no.45, 2019, pp.62–73

Jean Laurel Fredrickson, 'Gender and Deterritorialized Identity: Sonia Boyce, Latifa Echakhch and Zineb Sedira at the 59th Venice Biennale',

NKA *Journal of Contemporary African Art*, no.53, 2023, pp.74–87

John Roberts, 'Sonia Boyce: In Conversation with John Roberts', *Third Text*, no.1, 2008, pp.55–64

Nizan Shaked, 'Sonia Boyce: Reclassifying Classification', *Afterall*, vol.49, 2020, pp.27–36

Allison Thompson, 'Sonia Boyce and Crop Over', *Small Axe*, vol.13, no.2, 2009, pp.148–63

REFERENCE BOOKS

David A. Bailey, Ian Baucom and Sonia Boyce (eds), *Shades of Black: Assembling Black Arts in 1980s Britain*, London and Durham, NC 2002

David A. Bailey and Allison Thompson, *Liberation Begins in the Imagination: Writings on Caribbean-British Art*, London 2021

Rosemary Betterton (ed.), *Looking On: Images of Femininity in the Visual Arts and Media*, London 1987

Alice Correia (ed.), *What is Black Art?*, London 2022

Rebecca Fortnum (ed.), *Contemporary British Women Artists in their Own Words*, London 2010

Kobena Mercer, *Travel & See, Black Diaspora Art Since the 1980s*, Durham and London 2016

Rozsika Parker and Griselda Pollock, *Framing Feminism: Art and the Women's Liberation Movement 1970–85*, London 1987

James Putnam, *Art and Artifact: Artists and the Museum*, London 2000

INDEX

Page references in *italics*
indicate images.

CREDITS

First published 2024 by order of the Tate Trustees
by Tate Publishing, a division of Tate Enterprises Ltd
Millbank, London SW1P 4RG
www.tate.org.uk/publishing

A catalogue record for this book is available from
the British Library

ISBN 978 1 84976 950 1

Distributed in the United States and Canada by
ABRAMS, New York

Library of Congress Control Number applied for

Commissioning Editor: Emma Poulter
Editorial Assistant: Aki Gurung
Production: Juliette Dupire
Picture Researcher: Sarah Tucker
Design: Astrid Stavro Studio
Colour reproduction by DL Imaging, London
Printed and bound in Italy by Printer Trento S.r.l

Cover: *Untitled (Kiss)* 1995 (detail, see p.65)
Frontispiece: *Sonia Boyce* 2018. Photo:
Anne Purkiss

Measurements of artworks are given in
centimetres, height before width and depth

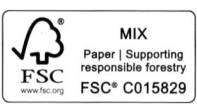

THE AUTHOR
Elena Crippa is a specialist in modern and
contemporary art, with a particular emphasis
on British art since 1945. In 2024, she joined The
Courtauld, London as Curator of Contemporary
Art. She was previously Head of Exhibitions at
London's Whitechapel Gallery and Senior Curator
of Modern and Contemporary Art at Tate Britain,
where her exhibitions explored transnational
and transcultural intersections and included *All
Too Human* (2018), *Frank Bowling* (2019), *Paula Rego*
(2021), and the 2022 commission *Hew Locke: The
Procession*.